Que este livro possa te lembrar os bons momentos vividos aqui. Lívia e Rafael.

"For visitors, figuring out how to relax and fit into this lar[...] provoke anxiety. Now there is an amusing guidebook f[...] writer based in Rio that helps ease the strain. *How to Be a* [...] much a compendium of tongue-in-cheek observations ab[...] hometown as it is a handbook for the newcomer."

You've learnt to be a carioca! —
But, ... please never forget! Kisse[...]

"Priscilla invented a genre and the result is very *maneiro* (in [...] those who don't know, the pronunciation is *mah 'nay rroo* . . . The book exposes *Carioca* whims through subtly accurate observations . . . *Carioca* humor at its best."

—*VEJA RIO* magazine

Jeremy
Você é um cara muito simpático! Abraços
Eliat

"MARVELOUS . . . A MASTERPIECE . . . THE BEST OF HUMOR."
—JÔ SOARES
humorist, talk-show host, and best-selling author

"*How to Be a Carioca* has become a best seller among the tourists who arrive in Rio thinking they are going to encounter parrots and sombreros in profusion."

—*JORNAL DO BRASIL*

"Complete with hilarious observations, *How to Be a Carioca* is pleasing the tourists as well as the *Cariocas,* surprised by the precise observations of their habits on the part of a foreigner."

—*O ESTADO DE SÃO PAULO*

You could try ... Be happy! Marcos Freitas

Você já é quase um carioca! E não é + branquinho ... Luisa

JEREMY O LIVRO É PARA VOCÊ SE LEMBRAR DA GENTE MAS VOCÊ JÁ É UM CARIOCA "DA GEMA". Márcia Fraga

"A sociological treatment about Rio de Janeiro has just been published and nobody realized it! No maps, no tourist routes. Instead, a commentary about the most incoherent city in the Milky Way galaxy ... A best seller has been born."

—*O GLOBO*

"For the majority of tourists, visiting Rio without calling attention to themselves is almost a mission impossible. But now they can count on a priceless manual: *How to Be a Carioca.*"

—*JORNAL DO COMMERCIO*

"The book of the moment . . . A result of well-humored, sociological observations, the book unmystifies in detail *Carioca* behavior for the benefit of unwitting foreign tourists."

—*HOTELNEWS* magazine

"The launching of *How to Be a Carioca* couldn't have been better for the author. On book-signing night, the first edition was already sold out."

—*JORNAL DO BRASIL*

"Priscilla . . . paints a well-humored picture of the city to help her fellow countrymen get around in Rio."

—*SUPERINTERESSANTE* magazine

"A SUCCESS . . . Much commented . . . a manual of tips for the foreign tourist who falls in love with the city and wants to better integrate with the *Carioca* way of being."

—*PAN-NOTAS* (weekly tourism newsletter)

"In love with Rio . . . Priscilla Ann Goslin, a resident for twenty-two years, has written a guide which bridges the gap between the tourist and the *Carioca.*"

—*MULHER DE HOJE* magazine

"Book by *gringa* which teaches tourists how to pass as *Cariocas* leads the pack of new books . . . Aimed primarily at *gringos* who want to avoid humiliating experiences . . . the most perfect translation of *carioquês.*"

—*O DIA*

HOW TO BE A
CARIOCA

ACKNOWLEDGEMENTS

Many thanks and much appreciation to Carlos Araújo for his editorial assistance; to John Gluck for his humor; to Amy Hunt for her proofreading; to Chick for his creativity; to Shane and Sundance for putting up with the madness; to Gary, Diana, and Pat for their feedback; to Carlão for being a *real* Carioca and without whom this book would never have been possible; and to my parents, Helen and Finley, for their love and support, but primarily for getting me to Rio in the first place.

Livros TwoCan Ltda.
Estrada da Gávea, 847 Lj 103 • 22610-000 Rio de Janeiro, RJ, Brasil
Tel/fax: (21) 3322-0314 • Web site: www.howtobe.com

All rights reserved, including the right to reproduce this book or portions thereof in any form whatsoever.

Todos os direitos reservados sob a legislação em vigor. É proibido reproduzir este livro, no todo ou em parte, a não ser após autorização específica e por escrito.

ISBN 85-85556-01-3
Copyright © 1991, 2002 by Priscilla Ann Goslin
Copyright of Illustrations ©1991, 2002 by Carlos Erymá Carneiro Filho

1st Edition: June 1992 / *1ª Edição: Junho 1992*
21st Printing: August 2002 / *21ª Edição: Agosto 2002*

Book Design/*Programação Visual* - **Priscilla Ann Goslin**
Desktop Publishing/*Editoração Eletrônica* - **J.C. Mello**
Printed by/*Impresso por*
Gráfica **JB** - Tel: (21) 3889-1609

Printed in Brazil/*Impresso no Brasil*

*To the hard-working Carioca
whose sense of humor
makes Rio such a delight*

A DICTIONARY DEFINITION —

CARIOCA [kah-rree-'aw-kah] *mf/adj* native of, pertaining to, Rio de Janeiro. Nickname given by the Indians to the first white men who came to live in Rio de Janeiro.

So you're flying down to Rio de Janeiro, right? Great! Being the sophisticated, self-confident traveler you are, you'll have the time of your life in the capital of fun in the sun. But whether you're flying in from New York, London, or anywhere else in the world, you won't want to act like a fool or a bumbling yokel from some unsophisticated foreign land when you get here, or people will stare at you and call you "gringo." Even worse, they might point and call you a tourist. Being the adventurous traveler you are, when in Rio, you'll want to blend in with the locals. You'll want to be a *Carioca!*

Whether you're a tourist or a local, it's no secret that all major cities have their problems. Recently, for example, while trying to hail a cab on a street corner in an obscure section of New York, a very friendly sort of fellow approached me and said, "Hey, d'ya wanna buy a watch?"

Seeing as they were real nice looking timepieces, I said, "Sure!"

The next thing I knew, he and my wallet were hightailing it down some dark alley. Talk about feeling like a fool.

For some reason, though, in spite of all its glory and splendor, Rio seems to be getting the short end of the stick. To make my point, consider this story I heard awhile back.

Three men were in an airplane: a New Yorker, a *Parisienne,* and a *Carioca.* The American put his hand out the window of the plane and said, "Ah, we are flying over New York."

The others asked, "How do you know?"

"I just touched the Statue of Liberty!"

A little while later the *Parisienne* put his hand out the window and sighed, "Ah, we are flying over Paris."

The others asked, "How do you know?"

"I just touched *zee* Eiffel Tower!"

A little while later the *Carioca* put his hand out the window and said, "Ah, we are flying over Rio."

The others asked, "How do you know?"

"Someone just stole my watch!"

Now a *Carioca* will be the first to laugh at himself, but this story is bad press in my book. Besides, I heard it from a *Paulista*—that's a local from São Paulo, the sprawling megalopolis an hour away as the crow flies, where loosening up and having a good time means sitting in traffic wearing a suit while passing out business cards to the other motorists stuck in their cars.

Anyway, you are about to visit, or are visiting, the most beautiful city in the world—the *Cidade Maravilhosa* (Marvelous City)—with its gorgeous beaches, breathtaking scenery, and above all, *Cariocas,* those stunning women and virile men who are lucky enough to reside in paradise. Which reminds me of a conversation between a *Gaúcho*—a local from Rio Grande do Sul—and a *Carioca* I overheard recently while having a few beers at a *boteco,* one of those charming little bars you find on most street corners in Rio. It went something like this.

"In the South," began the *Gaúcho,* "they say that if there were a fight involving a *Gaúcho,* a *Paulista,* a *Mineiro* (a local from Minas Gerais), and a *Carioca,* the *Gaúcho* would fight, the *Paulista* would get beaten up, and the *Mineiro* would try to separate the two."

"What about the *Carioca*?"

"He would have run away long before!"

I know it was in poor taste, but like I said, this one came from a *Gaúcho,* one of those Brazilian men from the South whose favorite pastime is sitting around sipping tea while boasting about their machismo. No *Carioca* macho I know would sit around sipping tea, that's for sure.

Well, you might be asking yourself by now, "Why do these otherwise worthy Brazilians feel the need to make stabbing jokes about the *Carioca*?" Well, that's obvious. They are all jealous—and I mean really jealous. Who could blame them? The *Carioca* has it all. They are witty, well-informed, playful, great looking, friendly, and sincere. Why, meet any *Carioca* and he'll say, *"Aparece em casa"* ("Come around to my place"), even if he hardly knows you. To top it all, aside from having the wildest Carnaval, Rio is home to the best soccer teams in the world. Ask any *Carioca,* and he'll agree with me on that.

So if you are visiting Rio, but don't want to stick out like a pair of wing-tipped, lace-up shoes in a room full of rubber sandals, read ***How to Be a Carioca***. Just a week or two of study and people will think you've lived in Rio all your life—and so will you. Soon you, too, will be feeling the joys of being a true *Carioca*. And remember, if you have any questions, don't hesitate—*"Aparece em casa."*

In attempting to create a comprehensive guidebook about the *Carioca,* those delightfully creative inhabitants of Rio de Janeiro, I think the author (with my generous input) has been quite successful. Believe me, if anyone can teach you how to be a local in Rio, she's got a clear shot at it. And since I am a legitimate *Carioca* from birth, you've got to give me credit for being an authority on the subject.

Of course, the art of being a *Carioca* incorporates millions of cultural peculiarities, well beyond those mentioned in this book. With enough ideas and material to fill a twelve volume encyclopedia, we came to the conclusion, being the good *Cariocas* we are, that it would simply be too much work. Therefore, we decided to do an abbreviated version and focus on giving you, the gringo, the opportunity to fully acquaint yourself with the positive energy that, thanks to the *Carioca,* radiates from this outrageously charming city.

We hope that in reading ***How to Be a Carioca*** you will get enough tips so that, like the *Carioca*, you'll always flow on a wave of good humor. Most importantly, while in Rio, just relax, take it easy, and you'll love it here just as we do. Besides, there is always time for another *choppinho* (an ice cold glass of draft beer) or two—*palavra de Carioca* (take it from a *Carioca).*

CONTENTS _____

HOW TO BE A
CARIOCA

Lesson 1

Taking Off

Paris, London, San Francisco, Rome, Buenos Aires, Tokyo, Madrid, New York, Rio de Janeiro? Rio? Yes, Rio.
  GREAT choice!

Lesson 2

Getting Started in Carioca

Being the seasoned traveler you are, you know there is more to a city than its sites. Namely, there are the people. And being the adventurous traveler you are, whether on vacation or business, you'll want to avoid making a spectacle out of yourself by acting like a tourist; you'll want to act like one of the locals. Therefore, when in Rio you'll want to be a Carioca!

Now there are Cariocas, and then there are Cariocas, but a *true* Carioca is a person who:

A. lives in the city of Rio de Janeiro, preferably on or near the beach (or else aspires to),

B. professes to being between 15 and 39 years old, and

C. makes it a habit of going to the beach before, after, or instead of work.

Note: All sexes, social classes, and ethnic groups are welcome.

Of course, you may be wondering if being a Carioca is for you. If so, find out by considering your willingness to do the following:

1. Substitute your pale, tense, competitive expression for a tanned look of confident serenity and complacency;
2. Trade in your plaid shirts, polyester shorts, and tasseled loafers for an Endless Summer T-shirt, surfer shorts, and a pair of rubber sandals, preferably blue;
3. Exchange your gold, initialed money clip for a rubber band;
4. Drop your third-generation, six-figure corporate name. (Dudu [Doo-'doo] and Betty ['Beh-tche] are more appropriate names than Edward and Elizabeth for someone who haggles with the local beer vendor on the beach.)

If you eagerly answered "yes" to the above and are ready to open your heart to the city of Rio, you are already on the road to becoming a true Carioca.

Arriving in Rio

Flying into Rio you will be landing at one of the world's most efficient airports. And it is at the airport where you will have your first opportunity to practice being a Carioca. Memorize the following essential words and phrases. They will help you get through those first scary hours at the airport. *Note:* Phonetic spelling has been used liberally throughout this book in order to guide the novice Carioca towards correct pronunciation.

 "E aí, mermão, beleza?" [ee ah 'ee merh 'mown beh 'leh zah]: "So what's up, buddy? Everything cool?"

"O negócio é o seguinte..."[oh nay 'gaw seeyoo eh oh say 'geen tche]: "The story is the following..."

"Num dá pra dá um jeitinho?" [noon 'dah prrah 'dah oon jay 'tchee nyoo]: "Isn't there a way around this?"

uma estupidamente gelada [oo mah eh 'shtoo pee dah 'mayn tche jeh 'lah dah]: an extremely cold beer.

At the airport: Upon arrival, disembark and proceed as follows:

1. Wait in the immigration line, get stamped in, and descend to the baggage claim area, which you will find empty.

2. Take a left or right (depending which airline you arrived on) and you will see a crowd rushing into the Duty Free Shop, the mecca for arriving Carioca travelers.

3. Follow the crowd, grab a shopping cart, and force your way through the crowd, filling your cart with the following:

- 1 microwave oven
- 1 case of imported Scotch or vodka
- 5 tubes of Crest toothpaste
- 1 package of Hershey Bars

(Of course, you probably won't need these items. But being a true Carioca you will always buy anything, as long as it is imported.)

4. Proceed to the checkout counter and wait in line.

5. After paying for your items, return to the baggage claim area and wait for your luggage.

6. Proceed with your cart, which contains your newly purchased items and you hope your luggage, to the customs line.

7. Wait in the customs line in order to press a large black button. If upon pressing this button you get:

A. lucky (a green light), proceed directly to the airport terminal, making your way through the sea of noisy awaiting relatives;

B. unlucky (a red light, followed by a honking sound), turn left into the customs inspection line, and wait for an agent to inspect your luggage. In the unfortunate event the customs agent finds an item he wishes you to pay duty on, simply proceed in the following manner:

Step 1. Create a friendly atmosphere by smiling before shaking the agent's hand when you meet him.

Step 2. Give him a thumbs-up and say:
"E aí mermão, beleza?"

Step 3. Pull out your previously prepared bogus receipt, pat him on the back and smile, saying:
"Aí, o negócio é o seguinte....."
(Your explanation should be dramatic, taking no less than four minutes.)

Step 4. Inquire as to the recent soccer scores and suggest discussing the issue at hand over **uma estupidamente gelada.**

Step 5. If you still haven't received the desired response, put on an innocent face and say:
"Num dá pra dá um jeitinho?"

(You may not get out of paying the duty charges, but it is always worth a try.)

The "jeitinho": The Carioca will *always* try to find some way around a problem. This attitude is second nature to a Carioca and is referred to as the **jeitinho** (the Brazilian knack of getting around anything).

Therefore, your first step to becoming a successful Carioca is learning to recognize situations in which you, too, can use the **jeitinho**. For future reference, the following are just a few examples of when resorting to the **jeitinho** might be appropriate:

- parking your car
- paying for a service
- looking for a rest room
- getting a job
- getting through lines

- dealing with the law
- resolving traffic problems
- taking a bus with no cash
- making a phone call
- getting a taxi at six p.m.

Essential Vocabulary
Words and Phrases

In order to best enjoy your stay in Rio, it is essential you understand the local dialect. Therefore, the most important step on the road to becoming a true Carioca is developing familiarity with the following vocabulary words and phrases. Throughout the lessons in this book, upon finding non-English words in **bold print**, refer back to this chapter for their definitions. Then learn to use them with fluency. By the way, the pronunciation is simple: where there is one "r" the sound will be "h" or "rrr," where there is a "te" say "tch," and always ignore the "h." Remember that many words have been spelled phonetically as a guide towards correct pronunciation. (Complete Carioca pronunciation rules on page 30.)

A

Aí [ah 'ee]: Hey! (As in *"Aí, me vê uma caipirinha."*: "Hey, give me a *caipirinha.*") Term used at the beginning of ninety percent of the sentences spoken by a Carioca.

A gente se vê [ah 'gen tche see 'veh]: See you.

alugar [ah loo 'gah]: to "rent" someone by talking too much and boring them. (As in *"Ela me alugou a noite toda."*: "She bored me all night .")

alucinante [ah loo see 'nan tche]: cool, awesome, excellent.

amarelar [ah mah rreh 'lah]: to chicken out of doing something daring.

Aparece em casa [ah pah 'rreh see eyn 'kah zah]: Show up at my place. (A phrase used by Cariocas when terminating a social encounter. *Note:*It should never be interpreted as an invitation.)

armar [ah 'mahrr]: to set up something (like a date or a trip).

B

babaca [bah 'bah kah]: a jerk.

baranga [bah 'rran gah]: woman with an unappealing body.

barzinho [bah 'zee nyoo]: small bar where Cariocas belly-up for a *cafezinho* or a shot of *cachaça*. See *boteco.*

boteco [booh 'teh koo]: Carioca fast-food joint. The same as a *barzinho* or *botequim*, but smaller, often having two tiny tables next to the bar.

botequim [booh tchee 'keen]: Carioca's favorite hang-out. Larger than a *boteco*, usually situated on a corner, and often having a few tables on the sidewalk.

bodibodin [baw gee 'baw geen]: water sport consisting of catching a wave with a body-sized compressed rubber board (body boarding).

bunda ['boon dah]: derriere. Watching women's *bundas* is a popular Carioca year-round sport.

busum [boo 'zoom]: city bus.

C

cachaça [kah 'shah sah]: Brazil's answer to kerosene and alcohol. Made from sugar cane, it is the basic ingredient in the Carioca's favorite drink. See *caipirinha.*

cadê [kah 'deh]: Where is...? (As in *"Cadê meu livro?"*: "Where is my book?")

caixote [kahee 'schaw tche]: big unsurfable wave.

camburão [come boo 'rrown] or **cambura**: police vehicle made for four policemen and with room in the back for eventually arrested criminals. Usually seen with six cops riding with their machine guns out the window. The "cage" (*caçapa*) on the back is made for two, but as many people as necessary can be shoved in.

caipirinha [kahee pee 'rreen nyah]: favorite Carioca drink; always followed by another. See *cachaça*.

camelô [kah meh 'loh]: street vendor.

caninha [kah 'neen nyah]: 1. police officer (cop); 2. the basic ingredient in the Carioca's favorite drink. Same as *cachaça*.

cara ['kah rrah]: a guy or man. (As in *"Aí, cara."*: "Hey, man.")

Caralho [kah 'rrah lyoo]: Holy cow!

cheques voadores ['sheh keysh voh ah 'doh rreesh]: flying checks which are covered the next day at the bank. A common weapon used by Cariocas in the battle against inflation.

chifrar [she 'frah]: to be unfaithful to your lover or spouse.

chinelos [she 'neh loosh]: slippers, flip-flops, go-aheads.

chocante [show 'cun tche]: see *alucinante*.

chopp ['showp] or **choppinho**: draft beer.

cerva ['seh vah]: bottled beer (short for *cerveja*).

Cidade Maravilhosa [see 'dah gee mah rrah vee 'lyoh zah]: Marvelous City; synonymous with Rio de Janeiro.

D

dançar [dun 'sah]: 1. to dance; 2. to get caught by the police doing something you were not supposed to.

dar um rolé [dah oon hoh 'leh]: go for a ride with no particular destination.

E

É mêrmo [eh 'meh moo]: Really?

F

Falou [fah 'low]: All right, OK.

fio dental ['fee yoh den 'tahl]: 1. dental floss; 2. string bikini.

Fique numa boa [fee kee noo mah 'bow ah]: Stay cool.

flanelinha [flah neh 'lee nyah]: dubious looking individual who will insist on watching your car for you while you are parked. A source of great irritation for the Carioca.

G

galera [gah 'leh rrah]: the group or crowd.

gata ['gah tah]: nice-looking woman.

gatinha [gah 'tchee nyah]: nice-looking girl (fifteen years old or less).

gato ['gah too]: nice-looking guy (thirty years old or less).

Gaúcho [gah 'oo shoo]: local from the state of Rio Grande do Sul. Males tend to think of themselves as very macho.

grana ['grruh nuh]: money.

guardador [guah dah 'doh]: see *flanelinha*.

H

Havaianas [ah vahe 'yah nash]: brand name synonymous with rubber sandals. See *chinelos*.

J

jeitinho [jay 'tchee nyoo]: the Brazilian knack of getting around anything.

K

kanga ['kun guh]: rectangular piece of material used by Carioca women as a bikini cover-up.

L

lambada [lum 'bah dah]: a popular sensuous dance originating in the Northeast in which two people move to the rhythm of the spirited music while seemingly glued together.

M

Macumba [mah 'koom bah]: "meal" consisting of a dead chicken, rice and toasted manioc flour, accompanied by a bottle of liquor and a half-smoked cigar. Served by candlelight, *Macumbas* are placed on street corners as offerings to the spirits, and will remain there untouched until a car or dog eventually runs across it making a real mess.

malhar [mah 'lyah]: to work out by doing physical exercise.

Maneiro [mah 'ney rroo]: Interesting...

mesada [may 'zah dah]: allowance given by parents to their kids which is intended to last a month's time but is spent in a week.

Me vê aí [mee veh ah 'ee]: Give me... (As in *"Me vê aí uma caipirinha."*: "Give me a *caipirinha*.")

mermão [merh 'mown]: my brother/buddy/pal/friend. (As in *"Aí mermão, não pode fumar aqui."*: "Hey buddy, you can't smoke here.") Usually preceded by the term *aí*.

Mineiro [mee 'nay rroo]: local from the state of Minas Gerais. Males are known for doing away with their wives to save their honor and defend their short calibers.

N

novela das oito [no 'veh la dah 'zoy too]: soap opera which Cariocas watch from 8:30 to 9:30 p.m. every night of the week. Favorite topic of conversation among many Cariocas.

Num dá pra dá um jeitinho [noon 'dah prrah 'dah oon jay 'tchee nyoo]: Isn't there a way around this?

O

Oi ['oooo eeee]: Hi! (A casual greeting among Cariocas; precedes a hand shake or some kissing.)

O negócio é o seguinte... [oh nay 'gaw seeyoo eh oh say 'geen tche]: The story is the following... (This term usually precedes a lie or a very complicated story simply put.)

P

pagar um mico [pah 'gah oon 'mee koo]: to be a fool or be made a fool.

parafina [pah rrah 'fee nah]: someone with bleached blond hair.

paraíba [pah rrah 'ee bah]: a hick.

Paulista [pow 'leesh tah]: a local from the state of São Paulo. Very sallow skinned, always seen in a suit speaking Portuguese with an irritating accent. *Paulistas* tend to address each other with the term *"O meu"*: "Hey, dude."

P.F. [peh 'ehff] **(prato feito)**: *botequim's* plate of the day, inevitably consisting of white rice, black beans, and beef jerky.

pirralho [pee 'rrah lyoo]: 1. irritating child; 2. people of short stature.

pisar na bola [pee 'zah nah 'baw lah]: to goof while undertaking a task.

pivete [pee 'veh tche]: thief under sixteen years of age. Very common, especially around the beaches or hotels.

Pô, aí ['poh ah 'ee]: C'mon. (As in politely, *"Pô, aí, dá pra pagar depois?"*: "C'mon, can I pay you later?") This term usually precedes a question or some whining.

Pô, que saco ['poh kee 'sah koo]: Boy, what a hassle! What a drag!

pochete [poe 'sheh tche]: device worn by Cariocas around the waist to carry pocket money, keys, and I.D.'s.

pa caralho [pah kah 'rrah lyoo]: a lot. (As in *"Tá chovendo pa caralho"*: "It's raining a lot.") Cariocas use this term *pa caralho* (all the time).

Q

Qualé [quah 'leh]: What's up? (As in *"Qualé, mermão?"*: "What's up, buddy?"; also *"Qualé a tua?"*: "What's the matter with you?")

Que gostosa [kee gosh 'taw zah]: How delicious! (Term often used by men when referring to a woman.)

R

rango ['hun goo]: food; also *rangar*: to eat.

ratear [ha tchee 'ah]: to steal from or fool someone.

rato ['ha too]: thief or schemer (male).

rato de praia ['ha too gee 'prah yeah]: beach thief.

S

saco ['sah koo]: 1. something that tests your patience; 2. a sack, specifically testicular.

sapatão [sah pah 'town]: 1. a big shoe; 2. a woman who prefers the company of other women.

simpatia [seen pah 'tchee yah]: a blessing used as a cure-all.

simpático [seen 'pah tchee koo]: nice, likable.

sunga ['soon gah]: Speedo-type bathing suit worn by Carioca men, whether they have the physique for it or not.

surfista [suh 'feesh tah]: 1. anybody who is or looks like a surfer; 2. some–one who rides waves or train tops.

T

Tá mal [tah 'mow]: a not-so-negative way of saying "no." (As in *"Vamu ao cinema?" "Tá mal."*: "Wanna go to the movies?" "No.")

Tá na boa [tah nah 'bow ah]: It's cool.

tanga ['tun gah]: tiny triangular pieces of material held together by strings. Worn by Carioca women as a bikini on the beach.

Te ligo [tchee 'lee goo]: I'll call you. (A favorite phrase used for terminating a Carioca social encounter, it means, in reality, "I won't call you."

transar [trun 'zah]: 1. have sex; 2. make a deal.

trocadinho [trroh kah 'geen yoo]: amount of money demanded by beggars from people on the street or in their cars.

U

Ué [oo 'eh]: Hmmm... (As in *"Ué, cadê meu sapato e minha meia?"*: "Hmmm, where are my shoes and socks?")

uma estupidamente gelada [oo mah eh 'shtoo pee dah 'mayn tche jeh 'lah dah]: an extremely cold beer.

uma gelada [oo mah jeh 'lah dah]: 1. an ice cold beer; 2. a dilemma.

uma lourinha [oo mah loy 'rree nyah]: 1. a cute blonde; 2. a beer. (As in *uma lourinha sem colarinho*: a beer without foam.)

V

Valeu [vah 'leyoo]: Thanks.

Vamu nessa ['vuh moo 'neh sah]: Let's go.

Vamu saí fora ['vuh moo sah ee 'faw rrah]: Let's get out of here.

Vamu sartá fora ['vuh moo sah tah 'faw rrah]: Let's beat it.

viado [vee 'yah doo]: males of a gentler persuasion.

Viu ['veeoo]: See? Got it? Understand? (As in *"Vou no show. Viu?"*: "I'm going to the show. Got it?")

Z

Zona Sul [zoh nah 'sool]: the southern part of the city of Rio. An area of the city where everything happens and where you'll want to be.

— HHH MMMMMM !... QUE GOSTOSA !!

SPEAKING CARIOCA

It's easy to sound like a Carioca. Just follow these simple rules, apply them with gusto, and you'll never be mistaken for a gringo in Rio—or anywhere else in Brazil, for that matter. By the way, most of the following phonetic sounds do not exist in English. Therefore, you might need the help of an authentic Carioca in order to master them correctly.

Rule 1. When a word has an "r" apply a guttural "h" sound (as if you were trying to clear your throat)

    A.   if "r" is the first letter in the word:
        As in **rato** ['**hhh**a too] = rat
                ridículo [**hhh**ee 'gee koo loo] = ridiculous
    B.   if "r" is the last letter in a syllable:
        As in **carta** ['ca**hhh** tah] = letter
                sorte ['so**hhh** tche] = luck
    C.   whenever you find two "r's" together:
        As in **carro** ['ca**hhh** oo] = car
                torrada [toh '**hhh**ah dah] = toast
    D.   if the "r" is the last letter in the word:
        As in **amor** [ah 'mo**hhh**] = love
                beber [beh 'be**hhh**] = to drink

Rule 2. Roll your "r" (as if you were freezing—"brrrrrrrr"—or perhaps imitating a galloping horse—"da rra rrum, da rra rrum, da rra rrum dum dum...")

    A.   when the "r" follows a consonant:
        As in **trânsito** ['**trrr**un zee too] = traffic
        Brasil [**Brrr**ah 'zeel]
    B.   if "r" is the first letter of any syllable (except for the first syllable):
        As in **barata** [bah '**rrr**ah tah] = cockroach
                caro ['kah **rrr**oo] = expensive

Rule 3. When a word has an "s" apply the "sh" sound (as if wanting to quiet someone with a "shhhhhh!")

    A.   when it preceeds a consonant (except for "c"):
        As in **gostosa** [go**shh** 'taw zah] = delicious
                especial [**shh**peh see 'yahl] = special

  B.   when pluralizing:
       As in **galinhas** [gah 'leen ya**shh**] = chickens
          motéis [moh 'tey**shh**] = motels

Rule 4. When a word has a "t" use the "tch" sound (like in "chit chat")
  A.   if the "t" preceeds an "e" in the last syllable of the word:
       As in **dente** ['den **tche**] = tooth
          assaltante [ah ssahl 'tun **tche**] = thief
  B.   when there is a "ti" or "te" sounds like "ti":
       As in **ti ti ti** [**tch**ee **tch**ee **tch**ee) = gossip
          Timóteo [**tch**ee 'moh **tch**ew] = Timothy

Rule 5. When a word has a "d" apply the "gee" sound (like in "gee whiz")
  A.   if the "d" preceeds an "i":
       As in **difícil** [**gee** 'fee seeyoo] = difficult
          dinheiro [**geen** yay 'rroo] = money
  B.   if the "d" preceeds an "e" in the last syllable:
       As in **cidade** [see 'dah **gee**] = city
          liberdade [lee beh 'dah **gee**] = freedom

Now practice your Carioca accent by repeating the following
sentence:

Vou passar um dia chocante na praia.
[voh pah 'sa**hhh** oon '**gee** yah **shh**o 'kun **tche** nah 'p**rrr**a yah] =
I'm going to spend an awesome day at the beach.

Lesson 5

Carioca Body Language

If your pronunciation is leaving you feeling a bit insecure, don't despair. Words are only a part of a Carioca's language. Incapable of speaking without continuous gesturing, the Carioca will use his arms, head, eyebrows, eyes, or the entire body to make a point or to ensure he has your full attention. Hands should always be in motion.

The following are a few examples of handy words and phrases with their accompanying gestures. Matching the words with the gestures isn't *that* important, as most gestures are interchangeable. Just keep those hands moving, and you will never be at a loss for words. (Refer to Lesson 4 for the correct pronunciations.)

"**Qualé a tua?**" ("What's the matter with you?"): Tilt your chin up, raise your eyebrows, move a step forward, and turn both palms upward in an inquisitive manner.

"**O negócio é o seguinte...**" ("The story is the following..."): Place your arm around the other person, slowly nod your head up and down affirmatively, and smile.

"**Vamu nessa**" ("Let's go"): Jerk your head to the side while moving your thumb in a hitch-hiking fashion.

"**Ué**" ("Hmmm"): Put your hand on your chin, then roll your shoulders forward and upward while opening your eyes as wide as possible.

"**Pô, que saco!**" ("Boy, what a hassle!"): If seated, slap your knees with both hands, stand up, take two steps forward, and then turn around before saying the phrase. If standing, throw both hands up several times in disgust while looking up before exclaiming, *"Pô, que saco!"*

Maneiro... (Interesting...): Slowly nod your head up and down, then smile very contentedly.

Body contact: Body contact is essential. If you want to carry on a conversation like a true Carioca, just stand as close as possible to the other person, maintain eye contact, and make body contact at least once for every sentence you utter. Acceptable forms of body contact when conversing with a Carioca are:

- jabbing the forearm
- caressing the upper arm
- tapping the shoulder or back
- patting the cheeks
- squeezing the hands
- poking the chest (men's only)

Body contact is never more important than when you greet another Carioca. Whether it's bumping into a friend on the street, joining a group of six for lunch, or walking into a party of twenty, it is imperative that you achieve body contact with each person individually, whether you know him or not.

For example, you walk into a restaurant and notice a friend having dinner with a group of people, all of whom you have never laid eyes on before. The following is the correct Carioca approach when greeting your friend:

1. Say "**Oi**" [oooo eeee] enthusiastically. This may be followed by "**Tudo bem?**" [too doo 'bayn]: "Everything OK?"
2. Kiss your friend on both cheeks (the right cheek first please).
3. Move around the table kissing each person present on both cheeks, regardless if that person has just taken a bite of his steak or is deep in conversation with the person seated in front of him.

Obs.: It is not necessary to make eye contact, or say your name or expect to hear theirs. As a general rule, women kiss women, women kiss men, and men kiss women. Men do *not* kiss men. The appropriate greeting between men is a handshake, followed by a few brisk, firm pats on the back with the left hand, then a prolonged lingering one-armed embrace.

Upon taking leave of this group, do the following:

1. Return to your friend and say, "**Tchau**" [chow] ("Bye").
2. Kiss your friend on both cheeks.
3. Move around the table kissing each person present on both cheeks. And remember: right cheek first!

CARIOCA TIME

There is British time, American time, German time, Japanese time, and Brazilian time (among others). And then there is Carioca time.

Try to follow a tight schedule or set important deadlines while in Rio, and you will soon discover that you're a candidate for an ulcer. Whether you've set up a business meeting, a dinner for six, a party for thirty, or simply a visit from the plumber to fix your kitchen sink, you will quickly realize that punctuality is not very high on the Carioca's totem pole. In fact, unless being late would result in dire circumstances (such as a missed flight), the true Carioca will simply ignore any predetermined schedule and will arrive for a meeting or an engagement at his own convenience.

Show up on time for a Carioca cocktail or dinner party and you will find yourself talking to the wall or spending an hour or so making small talk with an embarrassed hostess. And in this case, you can be sure your hostess' embarrassment was not caused by the tardiness of her other guests; she was simply not expecting your punctuality!

To avoid this sort of *faux pas* the next time you arrive on time for a Carioca "dinner-at-nine" party, instead of standing around alone examining the art in your host's living room, simply slip out the back door, and go (why not?) to a movie. That will give you at least a two hour delay, sufficient time to get you back to the party for your new entrance at eleven o'clock, and right on time with the other guests. And don't forget to pass by the nearest **boteco** for a few **coxinhas** or portions of **batata frita** (see Lesson 9, "Eating Out in Rio") after the movie to hold you over until dinner, which will be served punctually late.

THE CARIOCA NUANCE

Cariocas, by nature, tend to be extremely open, warm, and friendly. And to demonstrate their friendliness in social situations, you can be sure that they will never bid you farewell with a simple "good-bye." It would be just too dry and not in keeping with their nature. If you want to come off like a real Carioca, always terminate your social encounters with one of the following:

- "**A gente se vê.**": "See you."
- "**Te ligo.**": "I'll call you."
- "**Aparece em casa.**": "Show up at my place any time."

 But remember! These phrases are NOT meant to be taken literally or seriously. In other words, you are in agreement:

- "We WON'T be seeing each other again soon."
- "DON'T wait for my call."
- "DON'T show up at my place."

A real Carioca will use these phrases frequently and enthusiastically. But when they are directed at him, he will disregard them like a grain of sand on Ipanema beach. Therefore, follow up on any of the above phrases and you not only run the risk of feeling ridiculous, you stand a chance of losing your newly gained status as a local.

AND OTHER IDIOSYNCRASIES

As in most cultures, the Carioca has his little habits that, although perhaps frowned upon in other parts of the world, are practiced with great gusto on his own turf.

While waiting for a bus, having a **cafezinho**, standing in line, or catching a few rays at the beach—wherever—the Carioca male will habitually affirm his manhood by performing a continuous testicular jiggling routine. Beyond any scientific reasoning, this act is inevitably followed by an urge to spit, which the Carioca male will proceed to do in the most convenient spot available.

Dressing and Undressing

Now that you are speaking like a true Carioca, it's time you looked like one by dressing like one.

Dressing is an attitude, and nowhere will attitude influence attire as much as in Rio. Living in a casual city, a Carioca dresses for comfort, which is not to say that at any moment the importance of making a fashion statement is ignored. Whether it be a walk through the shopping center or down the streets of Ipanema, going to work, or simply going to the beach, a true Carioca is very aware of how he or she looks.

Ready to give up your Brooks Brothers suits, Coach bags, Ralph Lauren shirts, your Rolex watch, Burberry trench coat, and those Gucci shoes? How about your favorite rayons, polyesters, plaids, baggy shorts, and that bathing suit you bought last summer on the Islands? Good.

Your shopping list: The following are a few essential items you will want to pick up in Copacabana or at a local **camelô** (street vendor). Wear them with a flourish, and you will be on the road to looking like a true Carioca.

✓ For Her	✓ For Him
❑ skin-tight, low-cut jerseys (5)	❑ surfer T-shirts (5)
❑ plastic watch (1)	❑ surfer shorts (3)
❑ tight shorts or jean bermudas (2)	❑ **sungas** (2)
❑ form-fitting, mid-thigh skirts (3)	❑ jeans, one size too small (1)
❑ **tanga**-size, lacy underwear (5)	❑ **pochete** (1)
❑ **kangas** (2)	❑ **Havaianas** (1 pair)
❑ **tangas** (5)	❑ work-out attire (5)
❑ work-out attire (5)	❑ tennis shoes (1 pair)
❑ beach bag (1)	❑ diver's watch (1 imitation)
❑ costume jewelry (lots of it)	❑ dress shirt (1)

What to wear at the beach: *The* social area, the beach has a very specific dress code, and it is here the tourist's wardrobe tends to be a dead giveaway. Arriving completely dressed, the gringo will proceed to remove layers of clothing, only to expose a colorful, oversized swimsuit, offset by translu-

— HHHMMMMMMM !... QUE GOSTOSA !..

cent white skin. Please resist the temptation to do this. A few days at the local swimming pool can do wonders for that telltale glare. Ready to blend in with the locals? Try adhering to the following guidelines:

For Her: Wear as little as possible! The female Carioca arrives at the beach dressed in a Bali **kanga** rolled around her waist in the form of a skirt, with a T-shirt on top. After carefully selecting a spot on the beach, she skillfully proceeds to engage in an undressing ritual which may take up to four minutes, finally revealing a tiny, skimpy little **tanga**—thus leaving very little to the imagination. If you are a true Carioca woman, the bottom portion of your **tanga** should resemble a triangular postage stamp affixed to your tailbone. Opting for the more conservative look—by exposing only ninety percent of your buttocks—is also acceptable. Tugging, pulling, and repositioning these four triangular strips of material is a favorite activity while wearing a Carioca **tanga**. Note that there are no prerequisites as to shape, weight, or age when wearing a **tanga**. Don't be shy. All figures are entitled to bare all.

Made either of straw or plastic, the obligatory beach bag will contain an interesting variety of paraphernalia, all dispensable just in case some **rato de praia** (beach thief) comes along.

✓ Acceptable Carioca beach bag items

❏ tanning lotion	❏ dark glasses
❏ a couple of hair clips	❏ pen and paper
❏ a wooden comb	❏ pocket money
❏ the newspaper	❏ a hat
❏ lip balm	❏ smokes

For Him: Having the appropriate physique or not, Carioca men, young and old, wear Speedo-type bathing suits. Surfer shorts are also acceptable and worn by the surfer crowd, but note that they should be well-fitted and hang at least five finger lengths below the navel. Wearing baggy shorts in bright colors, you are sure to stand out like a neon sign. An old T-shirt and **Havaianas** are all you need to arrive at the beach in. Money for **cervas** and buses can be rolled into the lining of your shorts. Carioca men do *not* sit on towels. They shake themselves dry after swimming and always sit directly on the sand. Towels are for women, children, and wimps.

What to wear for business: Ten months out of the year Rio is hot. And for a couple of those months we're talking about the "fry-an-egg-on-the-sidewalk" type of hot. Obviously, since the Carioca would much rather be at the beach than at the office, he'll do his best to ignore this aspect of his life. But for those unavoidable hours when going to the office is on his schedule, the true Carioca will skillfully select the coolest and most comfortable items from his "professional" wardrobe for the trek downtown and back. It isn't uncommon for the more creative and spirited executive to keep his entire work wardrobe at the office. That way, by commuting on his motorcycle or in his air-conditioned car wearing shorts or jeans, tennis shoes, and a T-shirt, he simply arrives early at the office where the transformation to executive takes place behind his desk. By doing this, he avoids the danger of starting the day looking like he has gone a few rounds with the current heavyweight champ. This is the true spirit of a Carioca—comfort above all.

And those social engagements? In terms of dress codes, you will soon find that anything goes in this marvelously casual city. When lunch is on the agenda, perhaps the only rule which might be imposed by a Carioca eating establishment (save those restaurants which offer the finest in dining) is no bare feet or chests. Why? Who knows. But it's OK, ladies. No need to drag a shirt along to the beach. That itty-bitty **tanga** top will be enthusiastically welcomed!

If by chance you associate a night at the symphony with jewels and cummerbunds, go for it. Pull that tux out of moth balls and those rings out of the safe. Just don't be surprised if the fellow seated next to you at the symphony hall has opted for the casual look and is comfortably attired in shorts and **chinelos**.

At the gym: Since a large portion of time is spent at the beach, the true Carioca takes great care in getting into and keeping in shape. Therefore, at least one hour a day is spent at the local gym **malhando** [mah 'lyan doo] (working out). Seeing as the gym is also a social gathering place, correct attire is a must.

When choosing your Carioca work-out attire, you should start by picking out colors that glow in the dark, preferably pinks, greens, yellows, and turquoises. The better shape you are in, the more you should glow.

To show off those sculptured pecs, the guys will wear tank tops and shorts (no knee-length bermudas here). For the ladies, an infinite variety of combinations, such as halter tops, **tanga**-cut bottoms (wedged between the buttocks), and colorful tights—either in a shiny Lycra, or possibly even a see-through lace—will do. Be sure to have at least five variations in your wardrobe, one for each day of the week.

Just as it is at the beach, there is no discrimination as to shape; all figures are invited to indulge in the latest work-out fashions. So if even the thought of ten sit-ups tires you out, just find the nearest gym, look sexy, and you will fit right in.

Lesson 7

Dealing With Money

Looking good? Great. The next step is to put some **grana** (money) in your purse or pocket.

One of the more complicated aspects of everyday life while in Rio is definitely the local currency. Over the past decade Brazilian currency has changed from cruzeiros [krroo 'zay rroos] to cruzados to cruzados novos and back to cruzeiros, has dropped some zeros, and has added a few new bills and coins. If you are generally confused as to the value of bills and coins in Brazil, you had best pull them all out, lay them on a table, and begin studying. A true Carioca doesn't *ever* make mistakes when dealing with money.

Although Brazil's currency is the cruzeiro, just to complicate matters, you will also come across bills called cruzados novos. Due to inflation, these cruzado novo bills, although still in circulation, will eventually be negligible in value and will inevitably be phased out. It is important to note the five thousand cruzeiro bill, as it has two versions which differ in color, design, and artistic motifs. Both are still current and worth exactly the same thing!

Are you thoroughly confused with all this? That's OK. Just read on.

The true Carioca despises coins, will frequently refuse to accept them, and may even throw away any coin worth less than five cruzeiros in value. This includes the one cruzeiro, the fifty centavos, and the five centavos coins, all of which are often found littering the ground around bars, check-out counters, and the street corners. So if you want to act like the locals, toss a few coins over your shoulder the next time you make a purchase. It might even bring you luck!

Other currencies: Now that you are confident about the value of your bills and coins, it is necessary to understand what they are really worth.

Due to Brazil's inflationary economy, Rio is populated by approximately ten million economists. Although Cariocas seldom get their hands on the real thing, they are always up-to-date as to the daily dollar exchange rate on the official, tourist (used for buying dollars legally), and parallel markets in order to keep up with inflation.

Imagine, for example, that you have found a pair of shoes you can't live without in a local store. When you inquire as to the price, it will, of course, be quoted in cruzeiros. At this point, the Carioca will place his right index finger on his right cheek, roll his eyes, and ponder the issue at hand. By calculating the official exchange rate for that day, he will discover what the government stipulates the value of his cruzeiros to be in dollars, according to inflation. If calculated on the parallel rate, the real value of the shoes will be determined. If paid by credit card, it will cost a percentage more, but depending on the day the card payment is due, the Carioca might save a

substantial percentage off the asking price. There is always the option of making installment payments, in which case, hedging his bet on a maxidevaluation of the cruzeiro, he just might come out ahead. So how much did those shoes cost after all?

Consequently, the Carioca never really knows how much money he has or how much he is spending. He just knows that he is earning too little and spending too much and adjusts his life accordingly. A true Carioca will never have more than a little change in his pocket. At least three credit cards with different due dates and **cheques voadores** (flying checks) are the best weapons with which to fight inflation.

Remember: a real Carioca never despairs over financial matters. After all, there is nothing that a day at the beach can't cure. Besides, that is one thing that's free.

Lesson 8

Cariocas on Wheels

Now that you have a few bills in your pocket, it is time to get out and enjoy this beautiful city.

BY AUTOMOBILE

Have you ever dreamt you were behind the wheel of a Formula One race car, experiencing the thrill of overtaking another car by only a hair? Have you ever participated in a demolition derby? Great! You will feel right at home. Now is your chance to forget everything you ever knew about caution on the highways. Just keep in mind that driving in Rio is extremely fast, aggressive, and creative. Then put the pedal to the metal, and go for it!

The following are a few observations which might be useful to the novice—and not so novice—Rio motorist. Adopt them and you, too, will be driving like a true Carioca.

Speed Limits: Sure there are speed limits, but who's checking? When in Rio drive as fast as you like. You will not get stopped for speeding in the city, but always keep your eyes open since you are not the only one going over one hundred kilometers per hour!

Parking: Parking in Rio is "permitted" wherever there are no traffic policemen. (Downtown tends to be a little tricky!) It doesn't matter if it's on the sidewalk or in the middle of the street. Being a true Carioca you will simply deposit your car wherever it will fit.

Finding a convenient spot to deposit your car on the busy streets of Rio takes creativity. Therefore, in order to park like a true Carioca on wheels, it is absolutely imperative that you master the following acceptable Carioca parking methods:

1. The One-Wheel-on-the-Sidewalk Procedure
2. The Screw-the-Pedestrian Procedure
3. The Door-Dinging Procedure

ACCEPTABLE CARIOCA PARKING METHODS

1. ONE WHEEL ON THE SIDEWALK PROCEDURE

STREET

SIDEWALK

/////////// WALL OF HOME OR BUILDING ///////////

WHEN PARKING IN THIS MANNER LEAVE JUST ENOUGH SPACE FOR ONE AVERAGE SIZED PERSON ON SIDEWALK.

2. SCREW THE PEDESTRIAN PROCEDURE

STREET

SIDEWALK

//////// WALL OF HOME OR BUILDING ////////////

NAME SAYS IT ALL
NOTE: EXIT AND ENTRANCE TO CAR ONLY POSSIBLE THROUGH PASSENGER'S DOOR

3. THE DOOR DINGING PROCEDURE

VERY POPULAR IN SHOPPING MALL AND SUPERMARKET PARKING LOTS. LEAVE JUST BARELY ENOUGH SPACE TO SQUEEZE OUT OF THE CAR.

When your parked car blocks someone else's, it is a common courtesy to leave the parking brakes off. That way the blocked driver can simply push your car forward or backward, or bounce it sideways, thus making his exit. Just remember, if you are triple parked you might find your car sitting by itself in the middle of the street when you return.

When parking your car anywhere in this city, you may be approached by some dubious looking individual who will offer to look after (take care of) your car. This person is known as a **guardador**, or **flanelinha**, and can be easily identified by the flannel rag he'll be waving frantically, as well as his aggressive behavior. It is advisable to give him at least the equivalent of fifty cents in order to avoid any trouble. Giving him less than that or nothing may get him angry, and you'll run the risk of finding your car liberated of its antenna or scratched upon your return.

At night, in front of major night clubs or theaters, parking in a **flanelinha's** area might cost you the equivalent of US$10, although bargaining is acceptable. A true Carioca will go to great lengths to avoid paying a **flanelinha**.

Unless you are interested in subsidizing the car trade on the border, it is wise to always lock your car. The Carioca motorist will invest in several intricate locking systems and alarms in an effort to thwart even the most cunning and devious car thieves.

Traffic lights: One should always stop at red traffic lights, right? Yes, if it's a major intersection and it's daylight; wrong, if it's a minor intersection. In this case just slow down, check for oncoming traffic and cops, and go on through. After ten o'clock at night disregard *all* traffic lights at *all* intersections; just slow down, check for oncoming traffic, and take off! As is the case in most major cities, this traffic tactic is recommended due to the possibility of being approached by characters with unworthy intentions while stopped and distracted at any intersection, especially at night. No need to be a sitting duck, folks!

So you may be asking, "If everyone is running the red lights, what do I do at a green light?" Easy. At green lights apply the same tactic as you would at a red light, but just be sure to blink your high beams when approaching an intersection so other motorists will know you are coming through. The one who has the red light will *usually* give the green light the right of way.

Day or night, you will notice that there exist many red lights where Cariocas do not even hesitate—they fly right through. These lights are usually pedestrian crossings. The reasoning is simple: if there isn't a pedestrian in sight, why stop! Don't worry. In time you will learn when to stop, when to slow down, and when to breeze right on through a red light.

And the yellow light? That's easy. Speed up and make it through before it turns red. For sure, the car behind yours will!

General rules for the road: Lanes don't mean anything. Pass wherever there is a space and on either side. If you really want to drive like a true Carioca, never stay more than eight seconds in the same lane.

Squeezing someone is another way of saying, "Let me in." Do not squeeze a bus. It will gladly squeeze you back. Remember! No one pays any attention to blinkers—theirs or anyone else's.

By the number of cars on the road that have dings or dents, you might get the impression that Cariocas aren't very concerned about crashing. Not true. Just like anybody else, they do get very angry if somebody smashes or bumps into their car. The only difference in Rio is that if you were to leave your car at the repair shop every time you got a dent or bump, you'd eventually forget you had a car. Besides, what's a smashed fender or two?

Beware when the car in front of you signals that he is turning either left or right. Cariocas have a tendency to make wide turns in the opposite direction in which they are going, thus completely confusing those drivers who are following them.

Whether driving a car or riding in a taxi, a Carioca will seldom buckle up. Now don't for a minute think that the Carioca hasn't seriously weighed the pros and cons of this very sensitive issue. It's just that the cons seemed to tip the scale, and the following are a few reasons why:

1. If you were to accidentally drive your car off a bridge or a viaduct, you might drown;
2. If you were a taxi driver, it would be hard on the neck to turn around and talk to your passenger in the back seat while driving;
3. With all the time spent turning off the alarm systems every time you get behind the wheel, buckling up as well would mean you'd always be late;
4. It is just too hot. (Besides, it tickles the neck.)

The only time a real Carioca will wear a seat belt is when driving on a federal highway so as not to get a **multa** ['mool tah] (fine). Buckle up in the city and it is a dead giveaway that you're not a local.

Common courtesies in traffic: In Rio, it has been said that the shortest interval of time is between when the light turns green and the driver behind you honks. Since traffic lights are often hidden behind trees or strategically placed overhead at intersections, honking to let the driver in front of you know the light has changed is a common courtesy in traffic. Of course, it is always wise to double check before stepping on the gas. That honking motorist behind you might be just trying to catch the attention of a passing **gata** or **gatão**.

If the driver in front of you puts his hand out the window and motions in an open-and-close fashion, you can be sure he is not suggesting that you are talking too much. He is simply letting you know that you forgot to turn off your headlights after passing through a tunnel.

It is wise to always keep an eye on your rearview mirror. In the blink of an eye you will find a car, one that had previously been nowhere in sight, just centimeters from your rear bumper flashing his brights. This is the Carioca way of letting you know that you are expected to move over and let him pass. If you don't, he will just squeeze in next to you anyway and pass into the seemingly nonexistent space in front of you.

Although there are several acceptable Carioca procedures for parking your car in Rio, there is only *one* way a Carioca on wheels will pass a slower car when going through any of Rio's numerous tunnels.

The Correct Procedure For Passing in a Tunnel

Step 1. Tailgate the slower car in front of you by maintaining a maximum distance of five inches.

Step 2. Continuously blink your high beams (at least five times).

Step 3. Down shift one gear (fourth to third).

Step 4. Move aggressively to the *right* lane without using your blinker.

Step 5. Accelerate completely, **pé na tábua** (pedal to the metal)!

Step 6. As you are passing the slower car, signal your disgust to the other driver by tossing your hand in the air in his direction, shaking your head in disbelief, and uttering the appropriate language while shifting back into fourth.

Step 7. Once the pass is completed, move aggressively back to the *left* lane without using your blinker.

Step 8. Be sure not to leave more than three feet between your back bumper and the car you have just passed. If you leave more, another car will squeeze in behind your car and tailgate YOU.

When it seems like nobody is going to let you through when you're attempting to enter a speed lane, move out of a parking spot, or make a turn, use the "thumbs-up technique." Simply put your hand out of the car window in a thumb upward motion, smile, and go for it. The "thumbs-up technique" makes any maneuver acceptable.

A word of caution: Do not be tempted to use the traditional thumb and index finger OK sign when veering through Rio's traffic. Since the OK sign has a very different connotation in this country, when using it you might find yourself in a not-OK situation.

BY TAXICAB

If you are not sure about trying your hand at the wheel in Rio, try just going for the ride. By taxi you will live all the excitement of the traffic without having to drive. Best of all, if by any chance you do get in an accident, it won't be your car, and it won't be your fault either!

THUMBS UP TECHNIQUE

Cabs are painted yellow with a blue stripe. You will see small cabs and big cabs. They all cost the same, big or small. So if you are not in a hurry, pick out a decent-looking, bigger cab, preferably one with four doors—just in case you need to make a speedy exit.

To stop a cab, wave frivolously, but don't stand on the road. Due to the taxi driver's enthusiasm, he might run you over! Then get in and tell the driver where you want to go.

Never criticize a taxi driver's driving ability, even if he seems to be completely out of control. Carioca taxi drivers get very offended since they consider themselves the only good drivers on the road.

The meter will show numbers that do not represent the price. Due to constant inflation, drivers carry conversion tables to keep the fares up-to-date. There should also be one conveniently attached to the window of the rear seat for your own reference.

Talk to the driver about the weather or the traffic. Create a friendly atmosphere, and attempt not to look ignorant—or like a tourist. If you look like you don't know what you're doing, the conversion table will be left aside, and he will feel justified to create a "gringo surcharge" (in other words, rip you off)!

Real Cariocas will only take taxicabs in emergencies. A real Carioca will drive or take the bus.

THE BUS

If his car has been stolen, is in the shop, or if he just doesn't have one, the Carioca will look to the public transportation system as a convenient, dependable means of getting around. Consequently, when riding the bus in Rio, you'll have the opportunity to encounter Cariocas from all walks of life: from the executive who commutes on the bus to avoid dealing with the bother of downtown parking, to the **Dragão Chinês** (Chinese Dragon popsicle) salesman who gets on the bus in mid-summer with a styrofoam container filled with popsicles, sells them all to the passengers, and then, before jumping off, announces to his captive audience that he loves having been born a Carioca because he gets to make a living without having to *really* work.

Riding the bus gives you a different perspective on the traffic, plus plenty of room to admire the view. You'll feel a lot safer riding the bus,

but it is a fake sense of security since bus drivers race and squeeze each other just like everybody else does. Only by trying it can you experience and believe the speed and G-forces which can be achieved while riding on a public bus.

Buses will only stop at their bus stops, which are clearly marked by small wooden signs with numbers on them, either attached to poles by the road or hanging from nearby trees. The easiest way to spot a bus stop is to look for a gathering of people by the right side of the street, and there should be one every other block or so. *Note:* A real Carioca *can* manage to stop a bus away from the bus stop.

When picking up a passenger, some bus drivers tend to avoid coming to a complete stop, thus causing passengers to grab on and hop in while the bus is in motion. Since this requires running, jumping, and pulling, being in good athletic condition is strongly recommended before attempting your first bus ride around Rio.

It comes with the territory that when riding a bus in Rio you might have the opportunity to experience one of the city's most common inconveniences—you might be mugged. Unfortunately, that is a risk you take when riding a bus in any major city. And luckily, in Rio, it's really not that bad since muggers are only out for the loot (the cameras and expensive looking jewelry that could so easily have been left back at the hotel or your apartment), and they are really not interested in you. But if being pick-pocketed or robbed on a bus isn't your idea of a good time, it can definitely be avoided by not having any of the following in your possession while riding a local bus:

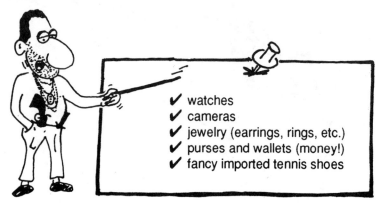

    ✔ watches
    ✔ cameras
    ✔ jewelry (earrings, rings, etc.)
    ✔ purses and wallets (money!)
    ✔ fancy imported tennis shoes

Since you'll obviously have to carry *some* cash, the Carioca thing to do is to keep it in two wads in your pocket: one for you and one for the thieves. Remember! Assault time is NO time for heroics! However, in the event you do happen to suffer one of these inconveniences, just remember to keep your wits about you and remain cool. Besides, it's a great topic for conversation later over a few **chopps** or **caipirinhas** back at your favorite **boteco**. (Refer to Lesson 9, "Eating Out in Rio.")

BY MOTORCYCLE

Cariocas on wheels tend to come within a hair of altering their existence, especially when the wheels they are negotiating through Rio's traffic belong to a motorcycle. Therefore, anyone with suicidal tendencies should try their hand at a motorcycle on the streets of this beautiful city. If you fit this description, it is recommended you look for a dirt bike, or any other similar kind of machine, due to the varying degrees of (or lack of) pavement you might encounter. Remember that you will be sharing the road with taxis, buses, and cars, so make sure you are familiar with this entire lesson in order to know what you're getting into!

The helmet is very popular among Rio bikers, although its use on the head is not. The helmet is usually seen attached to the rear seat of the bike—sometimes hanging to the left, sometimes to the right—or is carried on the arm of the rider. Contrary to bikers in other parts of the world who don protective leather gear, the Carioca biker will wear anything from **sungas** and **tangas** to business suits and party gowns.

The best thing about a motorcycle in Rio is its utility in rush hour traffic. By squeezing through the sea of motionless cars, or simply riding on the sidewalk, if you ride a motorcycle you are guaranteed to get to your destination well before any automobile driver.

ON FOOT

In order to appreciate Rio's natural magnificence and splendor, it is best to leave the wheels aside. Put on those shorts and **Havaianas**, roll up a few wads of bills and put them in your pocket, and enjoy the city on foot. However, sidewalks are often cracked or broken due to motorists who insist on parking on them, holes are common varying in size and depth, and dog mines are not unusual So a moment of distraction may result in an injury or a curb stop. Just remember to watch your step at all times (often making sight-seeing a bit hard on the neck), and then languish in the glory of Rio.

✔ **Obstacles to look out for while strolling Rio's sidewalks**

❑ dog mines   ❑ buses
❑ broken bottles   ❑ uncovered pot holes
❑ wood with rusty nails   ❑ automobile parts
❑ **camelôs**   ❑ bicycles
❑ sleeping beggars   ❑ motorcycles
❑ construction sites   ❑ parked cars
❑ UFO's (Unidentified Falling Objects)   ❑ **Macumbas**

Unless in search of a real adventure, a true Carioca will never walk the streets wearing or carrying anything of value. It just isn't common sense to do so anywhere in the world, unless, of course, your home town is Mountain Iron, Minnesota! But in the event some **pivete** (young street thief) should take a liking to your imitation diver's watch, simply smile and pass it over. The **camelô** you just tripped over should have another one just like it.

Pedestrian X-ings: You may have figured out by now that only animals have less priority than pedestrians when crossing a street in Rio. Remember! The Carioca motorist will make it a personal challenge to see just how close he can get to a pedestrian. If you want to cross a street like a real local, ignore all pedestrian overpasses and crosswalks when reaching a busy street. Just run for your life! And unless you want to be history, it's not advisable to attempt the "thumbs-up technique" when crossing a busy Rio street. You might end up facedown!

ASKING DIRECTIONS

Unfortunately, Rio is not known for its exemplary street signs, and even the truest of Cariocas will admit to occasionally getting lost. If you should find yourself in such a situation, do not become alarmed. Just stop the person closest to you and ask for directions.

Whether it be from your car window, at a bus stop, or on the sidewalk, Cariocas will always stop whatever they are doing to assist you. And you can be sure they will do so in an extremely accommodating and friendly fashion. A hand to the chin, a turn of the head in both directions, and a short pause will precede a lengthy series of intricate instructions on how to reach your destination, often accompanied by several options.

In the rare event that a Carioca is not familiar with the place you are looking for, he will take it upon himself to direct your question to the person standing closest to him, who will consequently ask another person. Soon a small crowd will form, at which time it is best to walk or drive away to try your luck elsewhere to avoid the ensuing chaos.

CARIOCA DEPARTMENT OF MOTOR
VEHICLES EXAMINATION

In order to find out if you would be safe behind the wheel in Rio, try taking the following multiple choice test.

Boa sorte! (Good luck!)

1. Before putting the key in the ignition, you should
   A. buckle up.   C. turn on the radio.
   B. check your gas gauge.   D. do none of the above.

2. If you reach a yellow light and the guy in front of you goes for it, you should
   A. prepare to stop.   C. note the car's license number
   B. accelerate and go for it.   and make a citizen's arrest.

3. How many car lengths should you maintain from the car in front of you for optimum safety?
   A. Five.   C. Half.
   B. Three.   D. None of the above.

4. When driving, you should never take your eyes off the road unless
   A. you see an incredible **gata** or **gatão** walking along the beach.
   B. you are looking for a parking space.
   C. you see the **pivete** that took your watch last week.
   D. None of the above.
   E. All of the above.

5. If a car has cut you off, you should
   A. ignore it and let him go.   C. catch up to him and tailgate
   B. cuss him out.   as you blink your high beams.

6. Besides the horn, what is the most important part of your car?
   A. The rearview mirror.   C. The back seat.
   B. The door knob.   D. None of the above.

7. Before obtaining a driver's license, you should
   A. go to a driving school.   C. make out your will.
   B. take out life insurance.   D. do all of the above.

8. When stuck in heavy traffic, you should
   A. call your wife on your cellular phone to tell her you'll be late.
   B. take a deep breath and put in that classical music tape.
   C. tune in to the seven o'clock news on your radio.
   D. do none of the above.

9. When you're speeding or illegally parked in Rio, your chances of getting a ticket are
   A. one hundred percent.   C. twenty-five percent.
   B. fifty percent.   D. none of the above.

10. When someone approaches you while you are stopped at a red light, they are probably going to ask you for
    A. **trocadinho**.   C. **trocadinho**.
    B. **trocadinho**.   D. all of the above.

11. When approaching a red light, you should
    A. check your watch.   C. run the light.
    B. stop.   D. wash your windshield.

Correct Answers to the C.D.M.V. Examination

1. **D** The first thing you should do when you get in your car is turn off your alarm systems and antitheft devices.
2. **B** Stop at a yellow light and you will have company in the front seat with you (in other words, the car behind you)!
3. **D** The only safe distance between you and the car in front of you is the distance behind you once you have passed it.
4. **E** Of course, you instinctively will look when seeing item **A**!
5. **C** Obviously. Be sure to flip him the bird on your way by.
6. **D** The padlock that locks your steering wheel to your pedals.
7. **D** Although, due to the red tape in getting one, a real Carioca will just end up buying one!
8. **D** Drive on the sidewalk while blinking your lights and honking to warn the pedestrians that you are coming through. Then enter the first one-way street, heading in the wrong direction.
9. **D** Between one and ten percent.
10. **D** You can bet your tangerines, lemons, lottery tickets, candy bars, air biscuits, and loose change on that!
11. **A** If you stop and it's after ten, you might be a sitting duck.

Check your score. Are you a real Carioca on wheels?

❑ All eleven correct and you are a natural Carioca on wheels. **Vamu nessa!** You'll be a Formula One driver in no time.

❑ If you managed to get six or more right, you're still a little wet behind the ears. **Calma, Bet-che!** (Relax, Betty!) Work on running a few more lights, and soon you'll be a tailgater, too.

❑ Got only between three and five correct? You'll be stuck in that traffic jam until the cows come home. Take a few tips from a taxi driver before getting behind the wheel again.

❑ Anything less and you should take the bus, pal.

Lesson 9

Eating Out in Rio

If you have decided that you are the adventurous type and are really getting into being a Carioca, eating out can definitely be an experience. Rio, the cosmopolitan city it is, offers a wide selection of excellent restaurants, and for special occasions you will find your own way to them. But being a real Carioca means that you will not go to the most expensive, and often the most snobbish, restaurant. You'll go to the one with the most atmosphere.

THE *BOTECO*

Teeming with atmosphere, the **boteco** (Carioca fast-food joint) is a small, stand-up bar with two or three tiny tables. Also referred to as a **botequim**, it is *not* the most hygienic of establishments. Cariocas will frequent at least one on a regular basis where they will get their mandatory **cafezinho** or have a quick **chopp**. Sometimes the Carioca will even go to a **boteco** for a quick snack where he will find a variety of very greasy delicacies to choose from. Among the most popular are:

coxinha de galinha [koh 'shee nyah gee gah 'lee nyah]: one or two tiny pieces of chicken rolled in a lot of dough with half of a chicken bone stuck inside—deep fried.

croquete de carne [kroh 'keh tche gee 'kah nee]: meat of dubious origin mixed with dough, usually rolled into a little ball—deep fried.

pastel de palmito [pah 'stehl gee pahl 'mee too]: small pasta pie with bits of hearts of palm floating inside—deep fried.

ovo cozido ['oh voh koh 'zee doo]: multicolored hard-boiled chicken eggs, often eaten in two bites.

P.F. [peh 'ehff] **prato feito**: ready-made house dish of the day, inevitably consisting of rice, black beans, beef jerky, and zucchini.

pizza: very soggy crust with a thin piece of cheese on top. Served at room temperature.

Obs.: The true Carioca will eat something even if it doesn't look very tasty. It becomes sort of a personal challenge.

In Rio you can eat just about anything—and I really mean anything. Sometimes you may not be sure of exactly what you are eating, so it's always best to have at least two **caipirinhas** before digging in. This not only gives you courage and opens your appetite, it kills any unwelcome micro-organisms which were not originally on the menu.

CAIPIRINHAS

Caipirinhas are the local cocktail, and a true Carioca will always have at least two of them at a sitting. Smash some limes in the bottom of a glass with several heaping tablespoons of sugar. Drop in some ice and fill the glass with **cachaça** (Brazil's answer to tequila and vodka), and you have the Carioca's favorite drink. Other variations include substituting the **cachaça** for rum (**caipiríssima**) or vodka (**caipirovska**), substituting the limes for grapes (**caipiruva**), or forgetting the fruit, sugar, and ice and having it straight up, which is referred to as a **branquinha** (little white one). Served with a **café com leite** (coffee with milk) chaser, it is a popular breakfast substitute for construction workers at the local **botequins**. Put **cachaça** and sugar together with any fruit in a blender, pass it through a sieve, and you have a **batida** (bah 'tchee dah). It's almost as much fun as a **caipirinha**, without all that garbage at the bottom of the glass to deal with. Have a few and you'll be dancing the samba in no time.

LET'S DO LUNCH!

Cariocas tend to go lightly on breakfast in order to save room for the lunch ritual. Downtown, during the week, lunch is eaten punctually at noon. Business people have their favorite lunch spots which are usually very small, hot, and crowded, with waiters who move like "The Flash," thus creating a rushed atmosphere. As a matter of fact, speaking of atmosphere, you'll find plenty in a typical downtown lunch spot. You won't find a salad or vegetable dish gracing these tables, though, as Cariocas seem to have a preference for pure starch. The only exception to this rule is when the sidewalk thermometers reach 40°C (104°F), and the **prato de verão** (summer plate)—which consists of a wide assortment of fruit together with ham and hard-boiled eggs—comes back on the menu. These heavy noontime meals are then burned off by standing in any number of bank lines in an effort to pay bills before heading back to another four or five hours at the office.

Of course, if you only have time for a stand-up-at-the-counter lunch, you will surely find a local **boteco** to meet your gastronomical needs.

The true Carioca will savor the **pernil** (pork roast) with pineapple sandwich or **coxinha de galinha** selected from the glass counter, but not before asking the fellow behind the counter, "**Tá bom isso aí?**" ("Is this good?") To which the fellow will most definitely reply, "**Ooo, tá ótimo. É de hoje!**" ("Oh, yes, very good. They are today's!"), even if they have been sitting in their juices for the better part of the week.

Lunch in areas other than downtown differs only in the respect that the suits, ties, shoes, socks, heels, stockings, and briefcases are back at home in the closet. In fact, in even the finer establishments in the **Zona Sul** section of Rio, one might see the clientele casually dressed in **tangas** (covered by **kangas**) and **sungas**.

On weekends Cariocas eat lunch anytime from noon until dusk, depending on the number of **caipirinhas** or **chopps** consumed. If you arrive at a restaurant for an early dinner, you will probably overlap with the lunch crowd.

FEIJOADA

Like all of us, you too may have always dreamed of eating a stew made of pig ears, tails, snout, tongue, and hoofs, combined with dried meats, sausages, slab bacon, salted pork, and black beans served on rice, accompanied by kale, fried manioc flour, oranges, and a **caipirinha**. Well, now is your chance.

Named by the slaves "way back when," the **feijoada** [feyh joo 'ah dah] is the Brazilian national dish and is traditionally eaten on Wednesdays and Saturdays for lunch. Be sure to put a spoonful of the accompanying **malagueta** [mah lah 'geh tah] (veeeeery hot pepper) sauce on top of the beans for that added adventure. Although **feijoadas** are served at the finest hotels and restaurants, a true Carioca will only eat a **feijoada** at his favorite **boteco**. And don't forget those **caipirinhas**!

If you should decide to indulge in a **feijoada**, be sure that you have the rest of the day free. Since the aftermath of eating a **feijoada** may be very dangerous, the following post-**feijoada** precautionary measures should be observed:

- *Do not* wear tight pants.
- *Do not* go out to play soccer.
- *Do not* operate heavy machinery.
- *Do not* have sex, wild or otherwise.

Acceptable options of things to do *after* eating a **feijoada** are:

- Lie in the hammock on the veranda or under a tree with your eyes closed, listening to the chirping of the birds.
- Extend yourself on a soft, comfortable sofa while listening to a Milton Nascimento tape with the air-conditioner at full blast.

DINNER

Cariocas won't even consider eating dinner until after nine o'clock, and most restaurants will serve until the wee hours of the morning. The fare will resemble that of lunch, although many will opt for a pizza or pasta dish for a change. Both lunch and dinner are preceded by the optional *couvert* (appetizers) consisting of the obligatory limp carrot and green pepper sticks, toasted day-old bread chips, and quail eggs. A favorite pastime while waiting for the main dish is identifying the contents of the various small stainless steel containers in which the *couvert* is served. Surprisingly, they are often excellent and tasty.

Rio has many eating establishments which offer a variety of atmospheres where you are sure to develop a taste for many new culinary delights. At the seafood restaurants which are located near the shore, you can eat just about every form of sea life from shrimp, crab, and octopus to squid and shark. **Casquinha de siri** [kah 'skee nyah gee see 'rree] (crab on a half shell) is a good appetizer. Try it. A true Carioca will ask the waiter first, though, as to the crab's origins, then disregard his answer, order another **caipirinha**, and enjoy!

THE *CHURRASCARIA RODÍZIO*

A favorite among the meat-loving Cariocas, these round robin steak houses offer you the unique opportunity of eating all the meat you can stuff inside yourself for one set price. It's traditional not to eat for the entire day, and then go to a **rodízio** and gorge.

A word of caution: Waiters make their rounds with lightning speed, and before you can say "**lingüiça**" [leen 'gwee suh] (sausage), the waiter will be offering you another cut of beef.

To avoid indigestion, it is recommended that you cover your plate with your hand until you are ready for that next sliver of meat. Although there does exist the danger of being stabbed in the hand when doing this, it is the only way to inform these speedy waiters that you need a chance to get caught up before the next round. A **churrascaria rodízio** [shoo 'hah skah 'rree yah ho 'gee zee yoo] is not recommended for vegetarians, dieters, or long-winded conversationalists.

THE *CAFEZINHO*

Cariocas run on caffeine. To enjoy a **cafezinho** [kah feh 'zee nyoo] (expresso) Carioca style, place a minimum of two heaping tablespoons of sugar in a tiny cup, pour thick black coffee over it, stir it into a paste, and down it in two sips. Consumed on an hourly basis at the local **boteco**, at the office, or after a meal, drinking a **cafezinho** is *the* Carioca ritual.

There are certain occasions throughout the Carioca's day when pausing for a **cafezinho** is imperative. The following are just a few:

- when bumping into a friend on the street
- after lunch and dinner
- when taking a few minutes off work
- when passing a place where good ones are served
- after drinking and before driving
- when checking out of a motel

BARZINHOS

Another option when looking for atmosphere, these are those cool little stand-up bars you'll find all around town. Similar to **botecos** and **botequins**, a **barzinho** will often have a few tables close to the bar or on the sidewalk. The larger **barzinhos** have substantial menus, but even though they may be lengthy, even a real Carioca will limit his order to **batata frita** (french fries), **aipim frito** (fried manioc root), and **bolinhos de bacalhau** (rolled codfish balls). **Barzinhos** are great spots to stop at when taking your date for a **caipirinha** or a quick **Guaraná** [gwah rrah 'nah], the Brazilian soft drink. By the way, made from the powder of an Amazonian nut, **Guaraná** is rumored to be an aphrodisiac. Hmmm...

WAITERS

While dining out Carioca style, don't expect the waiters to be perfect specimens of etiquette. They may stack the plates like the Tower of Babel, but they do have good intentions.

No cute outfits with striped hats and bar aprons here. Always fully dressed in a long-sleeve shirt, white jacket, and black bow tie, even when the temperature soars to 42°C (107°F), it is no wonder the Carioca waiter occasionally gets out of sorts.

If you are fortunate enough to find a good waiter in a restaurant you like, be sure to ask his name. That way you'll be guaranteed a few **saideiras** [sahee 'day rrahs] (drinks served on the house while waiting for the bill).

MENUS

Carioca menus tend to be lengthy, often four to six pages long, and due to inflation, the prices are either handwritten in pencil or typed on strips of paper, which are then pasted over the previous prices. The beauty of the Carioca restaurant is that, regardless of the menu, you can usually have any dish you want, prepared in whichever manner tickles your fancy, accompanied by whatever is available in the kitchen.

No matter how hard the Carioca waiter tries to please you, though, there are certain dishes you won't find on any Carioca menu (unless, perhaps, you check into a five star hotel). For example:

- tuna on white
- macaroni and cheese
- lemon chiffon pie
- cottage cheese with peaches
- root beer
- two eggs, over easy, with hash browns

- bologna on rye
- Rueben sandwich
- blueberry cheese cake
- Thousand Island dressing
- decaffeinated coffee
- buckwheat pancakes with your choice of syrup

In compensation, though, you might discover some other exotic dishes on the bi-lingual menus which you'll find in the finer food establishments, conveniently available for their English speaking patrons.

Carne desfiada com molho de ervilhas
(Meat Unwoven with Pea Cream)

Frango Alemão
(Chicken at Germany Mood)

Filet à Cavalo
(Steak Riding a Horse)

Filet ao molho madeira
(Steak with Wooden Sauce)

Frango com purê de batata
(Chicken with Smashed Potatoes)

Arroz à Grega
(Grease Rice)

Pickles
(Olivers)

WHAT YOU *WILL* FIND IN A CARIOCA RESTAURANT
Purple phosphorescent fly zappers.
A sink in the back of the dining area with an accordion stack of
coarse paper towels for drying hands.
Small wooden, hard-back chairs with one leg inevitably
shorter than the others.
Creative, plastic covered bi-lingual menus at least six pages long.
Rest rooms with the initial "S" on both doors, accompanied by
a subtle, indecipherable drawing.
Well-meaning waiters who seem to have inherited their white jackets
from slimmer predecessors.
Well-used, two-sided tablecloths, sometimes accompanied by
a plastic or paper covering.
Tables with a matchbox under one leg to balance them.
An occasional cockroach.
Forks with bent prongs.

WHAT YOU *WON'T* FIND IN A CARIOCA RESTAURANT
Cloth place mats.
Waitresses wearing white dresses and aprons saying,
"Have a nice day."
Waiters who identify themselves by saying, "Hi, I'm Brian, and I will be
your server today."
Waiters informing you of the "Catch of the Day."
Fresh baked pies and gelatin desserts displayed in glass cases.
Bills inscribed with "Please pay at register."
Menus from which you order by the number.
A nonsmoking section.

Lesson 10

The Carioca Summer

Those summer months in Rio, from September to May, are very popular because of all the available activities and the hot, humid weather. Summer also seems to bring out the inherent passion which lives inside all Cariocas, so the days when the thermometers reach 44°C (that's about 111°F, folks) are not really that bad—as long as you know what to do and what not to do.

What to do	**What NOT to do**
Go to the beach	Go to work
Sit in an air-conditioned room	Walk downtown
Drink **chopps** at the **boteco**	Drive during rush hour
Wear a **tanga** or **sunga** all day	Shop in Copacabana
Go to an air-conditioned motel	Wear much clothing

GOING TO THE BEACH

If you think that going to the beach is simply a matter of putting on a bathing suit, grabbing a towel, and heading for the nearest stretch of white sand to bag a few rays, think again. To the Carioca, going to the beach is an art form.

Before venturing out, be sure to refer back to Lesson 6 to ensure you are dressed (or undressed) appropriately. Then check your newspaper to see if the health authorities have liberated your favorite beach for swimming. Being a Carioca, ignore the warnings; but once your are there, do look out for:

- **pivetes** and **ratos de praia**
- fishing lines
- bugs that you can see and that bite
- bugs that you can't see and that bite
- UFO's (Unidentified Floating Objects)
- IFO's (Identified Floating Objects)
- dog mines

When in Rio, it is absolutely imperative that you go to the beach like a true Carioca. If you resort to your usual habits, you will definitely be labeled a tourist. Therefore, memorize the following thirteen easy steps on how to conduct yourself once you have arrived AT the beach. Remember! Your status as a Carioca will depend on it.

Step 1. Parking: When arriving by car you will naturally be met by a **flanelinha**, with the exception that here he will be waving not only a rag; he will be flapping a piece of cardboard at you while directing you to the nearest parking space. The cardboard is to cover your windshield so that you won't burn your fingers on the steering wheel after it bakes in the hot sun. Clever, no? Insist that the cardboard isn't necessary, and he will put one on your car anyway. Be sure to carry the appropriate change for him.

But before leaving your vehicle in his care, be sure to say:

 "**Te pago na volta, mermão.**" [tchee 'pah goh nah 'vohl tah merh 'mown]: "I'll pay you later, buddy."

Step 2. Collecting your paraphernalia: A true Carioca will always carry beach chairs, an umbrella, **esteiras** [eh 'shtay rrahs] (straw mats), and other beach paraphernalia in the trunk of his car. That way, no matter where he is, he will be prepared to stop what he is doing and hit the beach. (Of course, wearing beach attire from morning until the sun goes down always facilitates matters when the beach is calling.)

Step 3. Deciding where to sit: In the process of developing your new status as a Carioca, where you settle on the beach is of utmost importance. Sitting close to a beer vendor guarantees that your **cervas** and your **água com gás** ['ah gwah kown 'gaiysh] (bottled sparkling water) will be delivered ice cold, and you won't have to move from your spot when it comes time to order the next round. Avoid sitting next to the sewers or too close to the water. It is very embarrassing when a wave washes away your belongings, and it could even trigger an early departure from the beach. Of course, sitting close to the sidewalk where the sand is the hottest you run the risk of burning your feet going to and from the water. When sitting near the sidewalk on São Conrado beach, there also exists the added excitement of hang gliders landing on top of you. If in doubt, just check where the other Cariocas are, mark your spot, and join the crowd.

Step 4. Setting up your umbrella: To properly set up your **guarda sol** (beach umbrella), take the bottom half of the pole and stab it into the sand as hard as you can. Be sure to pay close attention to the direction of the sun to avoid repeating the entire process. Then rotate the pole in a counterclockwise motion, as if you were stirring a large pot of beans. Once it is securely buried—at least twenty centimeters in the sand—you are then ready to attach the top portion of your umbrella. (Reserve at least five minutes for this process. If you don't bury the pole sufficiently, it will fly away with the first gust of wind.)

On those crowded summer days, the color of your umbrella will be the only means in which to find your way back to your spot. Keep this in mind when purchasing your new umbrella. Consequently, the least attractive one you can find is a sure bet. (Perhaps a lime green with orange polka dots?)

Step 5. Laying down your towel or straw mat (only for women): Once again, carefully check the sun's direction before laying down your towel or **esteira**. Then prepare the sand in the following fashion: While standing, dig a hole in the sand with one foot, pushing the sand into a mound. The hole in the sand will cradle your bottom in a hammock fashion, and the mound will secure your head. Once you have built a substantial mound, smooth it over with your foot. Hand use must be avoided in this process. Place your towel on top. While lying in this position you are guaranteed a perfect view of all the sights.

Step 6. Getting settled: Once your umbrella is up, your chairs are unfolded, and your towel is down, you are then free to remove your "arriving-at-the-beach" attire.

For females: If you are not using a towel, unwrap your **kanga** very carefully and place it, with one snapping motion and a bend at the waist, on the previously prepared mounds. Next, remove your T-shirt, adjust the top portion of your **tanga**, and place your shirt, neatly folded, in your beach bag. Remove suntan oil from your bag, and slowly, *while standing*, spread it over your entire body. This should take no less than three minutes in order to achieve the maximum desired effect. Place your beach bag within easy reach, sit on your **kanga**, swivel at the waist, and stretch out. Presto! You are now ready to receive those penetrating rays. In order to prevent back strain when it is time to flip over, ask the closest **gatão** to oil those hard to reach areas. There should be an abundant supply of volunteers to help you avoid getting a nasty burn in those inconvenient spots.

👉 **For males:** Quickly remove your T-shirt and outer shorts, and hang them inside the umbrella. The longer you remain with your shirt on the less you'll look like a Carioca.

Step 7. Making friends with the beer vendor: Develop a friendly rapport with the closest **barraqueiro** [bah hah 'kay rroo] (beer vendor with his own stand). This may be achieved by first introducing yourself in the following fashion:

👉 **"Qualé mermão? Beleza? "** [quah 'leh merh 'mown beh'leh zah]: "What's up, buddy? Everything cool?"

Shake his hand, pat him on the back, give him the thumbs-up, and it will be the beginning of a great relationship. Be sure to indicate where you are seated, and he will keep those **cervas** coming. Don't worry about digging into the lining of your shorts or your beach bag every time you feel thirsty. Your running tab will be settled when you make that first move to leave the beach. A true Carioca's tab will be settled on a weekly basis. If you should opt for the weekly, or even monthly, tab—remember that beer vendors are also economists—your tab will most likely be adjusted on a daily basis according to the rate of inflation.

Step 8. Going for a dip: Eventually, after a few beers and your skin begins to feel crispy, it will be time to go for a swim. How quickly you get wet will be directly influenced by the water temperature and the number of beers and bottles of mineral water you have consumed.

Correct Procedure for Taking a Dip (for females)

1. Walk slowly down to the shoreline, continuously adjusting the bottom of your **tanga.**
2. Test the temperature of the water by getting your feet wet.
3. Between waves, walk in up to your knees and squat down far enough to just barely wet your buttocks.
4. Readjust your **tanga.**
5. When the next wave approaches, hold your nose and dive under it, making sure to get back to the shoreline as quickly as possible before the next wave hits.
6. Readjust your **tanga.**
7. Bend over at the waist and throw your hair backwards and forwards three times to remove excess moisture.
8. Readjust your **tanga** while slowly returning to your spot.

Correct Procedure When Going for a Swim (for males)

1. Run to the shoreline and dive (or flip) into the ocean without stopping to consider the water temperature or the waves.
2. Body surf or swim for at least twenty minutes.
3. Stop at the shoreline to adjust your equipment. Then shake your hair back and forth to remove excess moisture. (This is also helpful in avoiding that "wet seal" look.)
4. Run back to your spot.
5. Although you are wet, don't be tempted to sit in your chair. A male Carioca will always sit in the sand.

Step 9. Getting active: Now that you are fully energized after your swim, it is time to get active.

On a typical summer day, tens of thousands of Cariocas battle for their rightful place in the sun, on the sand, and in the water. This crowded scenario offers optimum conditions in which to indulge in the many beach activities available to the Carioca. You, too, can participate as long as you play by the rules.

The following are just a few of the beach activities available on a typical summer day in Rio:

• **Surfando:** Very popular around the world, this sport, also known as **pegando onda** (catching waves), takes on new meaning on the beaches of Rio. Riding down a wave while standing on a surfboard, the Carioca **surfista** will attempt to run over as many objects in his path as possible. Priority should be given to **bodiboders** and body surfers.

• **Bodibodin:** Also a very popular water sport, **bodibodin** differs from surfing in that the wave is caught while lying down on a body-sized, compressed rubber board. A **bodiboder's** favorite targets are body surfers and other bathers. It is important to note that running over a surfer while **bodibodin** is the equivalent of signing your own death sentence, the only exception being if the **bodiboder** is a she.

• **Pelada:** A form of soccer, **pelada** (meaning "nude") is played with at least two people. Carioca men are very serious about playing **pelada** and will always find a way to participate, even if it means hobbling around on a broken or bandaged foot. The object of this game is to kick a soccer ball back and forth through the beach crowd. As more players are attracted to the game, teams can be formed and goals made by positioning **chinelos** (rubber sandals) approximately two feet apart. On crowded days the chances of throwing sand on bathers and hitting them with the ball is greatest, and so is the fun.

• **Frescobol:** Reserved for those most crowded summer days, this racquet game is played on the shoreline where the sand is the firmest, and there is sure to be a constant flux of people walking by. Two players, each with a wooden racquet, stand approximately six feet apart and proceed to hit a small rubber ball as hard as they can back and forth, bouncing off as many people as possible without touching the sand.

• **Volei:** The only beach sport in which the participants actually pick an area furthest from the crowds, a skilled Carioca **volei** (volleyball) player will manage to include those bathers who are arriving or leaving the beach as his unsuspecting targets.

• **Olha a asa!** (Watch out for the hang glider!): Primarily played in São Conrado at Pepino (cucumber) Beach, this "bather participation" activity is also available on Ipanema, Leblon, and Barra beaches, although on a smaller scale. Excellent for those days when you go solo to the beach, all you need to do is get comfortable, close your eyes, and listen for the password. When you hear "**Olha a asa!**" jump up, cover your head, then run towards the ocean.

• **Body watching:** The all-time favorite pastime for Cariocas any-where, it takes on a whole new meaning at the beach (for obvious reasons)! All you need in order to play is a pair of dark glasses (optional for more discretion). The bodies are courtesy of the One Up Above, who, if you didn't know by now, is also a Carioca. *Obs.:* There is a definite danger of whiplash while indulging in this game.

• **Rangando** (eating): After so much activity you need never go hungry while at the beach, and the enormous number of beach vendors trampling around you will make sure you don't forget it. Some beach delicacies which are available to choose from are:

o natural [o nah too 'rrahl]: natural sandwiches
x-burger [shees 'boorr geh]: not-so-natural sandwiches
coco gelado ['koh koh jay 'lah doo]: chilled coconuts
sorvete [soh 'veh tche]: ice cream
cuscuz [kooz 'kooz]: coconut pudding
cachorro quente [kah 'shoh hoh 'ken tche]: hot dogs
amendoim torrado [men dooeen toh 'ha doo]: roasted peanuts
picolé do China [pee ko 'leh doo 'shee nah]: Chinese popsicles
mate e limão ['mah tche lee 'mown]: iced tea with lemon
saladinha de fruta [sah lah 'gee nyah gee 'froo tah]: fruit salad
melancia [meh lan 'see yah]: watermelon

The all-time favorite, though, amongst the truest of Cariocas is the **biscoito de polvilho** [beesh 'koy too gee poh 'vee lyoh] (air biscuit). These air biscuits are sold in packages of ten and come in two flavors—sweet and salty. What contributes to the success of this air biscuit is the mystery as to what it really is. Taking a bite of an air biscuit is like taking a bite of nothing, and the difference between the sweet and the salty is yet to be discerned. It is a good idea to eat these air biscuits accompanied by an ice cold **cerva**. Avoid eating them, though, when you are deep in conversation.

Step 10. Etiquette: If you think bumming a smoke, asking for a light, reading someone else's newspaper, asking others to watch your belongings while you take a dip, borrowing suntan lotion and asking the person to rub it on your back are not examples of acceptable behavior at the beach, wake up and smell the coffee! How else would you ever approach that gorgeous **gata** or **gatão**?

Step 11. Meeting friends: When bumping into someone you frequently see at the beach, you should always achieve body contact (refer to Lesson 5, "Carioca Body Language") before saying:

☞   "**E aí,** (insert person's name), **beleza?**": "So how's it going, great?" or " **Opa, e aí?**": "Hey, so what's up?"

Your response should always be affirmative, even if your dog has just died. Acceptable conversation topics may range from the weather to the most recent episode on the **novela das oito.**

Step 12. A galera da praia [ah gah 'leh rrah dah 'prrah yah]: After spending a few days at the beach and borrowing as many objects as possible, you will have acquired a group of acquaintances. These newly found friends are your **galera da praia** (beach crowd). A true Carioca will maintain a close relationship with the **galera da praia** *as long as there is sand under foot.* Remember: if anyone from your **galera da praia** bids you farewell by saying, "**Aparece em casa,**" resist the temptation to follow up on the offer without confirming by telephone first, even if they set a specific date. (If you do, you'll probably be met with a stunned look, and you will end up blowing your cover as a local! Refer to Lesson 5, "Carioca Body Language.") Before leaving the beach, be sure to embrace or kiss everyone on the cheek, saying:

"**A gente se vê.**" [ah 'gen tche see 'veh]: "See you around."

Step 13. When it's time to leave: When the sun sets either behind the mountains or over the horizon is the only truly acceptable time for a Carioca to leave the beach. Shake out your towels; close up your beach chairs; shut and disassemble your umbrella; put on those T-shirts, shorts and **kangas**; place all assorted items in the beach bag; kiss the **galera** and tell each of them you'll be calling; and pay off the tab with your new buddy—the beer vendor. (Don't forget to give him a firm pat on the back and a thumbs-up!) Then head slowly for the sidewalk. When you are within five feet of your car, quicken your pace, throw everything in the trunk, remove the cardboard from your windshield, and drive off as quickly as possible. Don't worry. The **flanelinha** will only chase you for a few meters, or until he sees another **freguês** [freh 'gaysh] (customer) pulling out. Then head to your favorite **boteco** for another round with your **galera do boteco** (bar crowd).

OTHER SUMMER ACTIVITIES

Submarine driving: Due to the intense humidity in the summer months, Rio is subject to sudden heavy rains. These deluges seldom last over thirty minutes, and unless you live on a hill or in a valley, they are merely an inconvenience. Naturally, there are a few recommendations to be heeded if you should unfortunately find yourself outside your residence when it rains in Rio:

1. If you have any experience piloting submarines, you shouldn't have any problem driving your car in Rio when it rains. A Carioca will drive through a flooded road as long as the water level does not go past his windshield. In order to avoid problems in this situation, just keep the clutch depressed with one foot, accelerate continuously with the other, while keeping the other foot (?!) on the brake. That way you won't float into the car in front of you, water will not enter your exhaust pipe, and you will save yourself the tremendous headache of dry cleaning expenses.

2. Be sure to keep your windows closed. If you don't, you might get caught by surprise by a tidal wave produced by a bus. And if you're not careful and the flood water level should reach the window, your car will sink, consequently ruining your tapes.

3. If the currents begin to take your car, don't panic. Just climb on top of your car and reach for the nearest passing tree branch. Then wait for the first person to come around with a boat or a surfboard.

4. Look out for snakes, leeches, rats, and "who knows whats" which often appear on flooded streets.

5. Be on the lookout for "flood pirates," and do not accept any offers for assistance. If anyone should offer to help, it will probably be a set-up, and you could find yourself minus your possessions and your floating device (your car).

6. If you should be on a bus, great. It is the safest and driest place to be, and it is where you will remain for the next few hours, crammed together with one hundred and ten other people.

7. If you find yourself in traffic when the rains hit, stop at the highest point on the road, lock your car, and have a few **chopps**, perhaps accompanied by a portion of **batata frita**, at the nearest **boteco**. Remember to have a **cafezinho** before returning to your car.

8. If you should be walking in the street when the rains hit, find the nearest dry **boteco** and have a few **chopps**—why not make that a few **caipirinhas**! You won't be going anywhere anyway.

Leaving town: The true Carioca loves to travel and will even concede his spot on the beach in order to do so. Any of the beautiful beaches along Rio's coastline—or Brazil's, for that matter—are favorite Carioca destinations. As far as the Carioca is concerned, though, **Paulistas** don't know "diddlee squat" about the art of going to the beach. And for that reason, as a matter of principle, a true Carioca will bypass any of the spectacular São Paulo beaches on his vacation if the **Paulistas**, those locals from his neighboring rival state, are already there.

Lesson 11

Carnaval à Carioca

Summer is Carnaval time, the Carioca's (and the world's!) biggest, wildest, best-known party, and all of Rio swings to the rhythm of the samba. Although Carnaval is officially in February, it is around New Year's Day when the Cariocas develop the sudden urge to dance the samba.

By beating on whatever is available—tables, pans, matchboxes, beer bottles, glasses, themselves—the Carioca creates a continuous, hypnotic rhythm known as the **batucada** (bah chew 'kah dah). You will see and hear **batucadas** being spontaneously created on buses, at street corners, on the beach, but most often in the **barzinhos** or **botecos** where there is a constant flow of **cervas** or **chopps** to keep the **batucada** and samba alive.

To enjoy the madness of Carnaval to its fullest, it is essential that you learn how to dance the samba.

How to dance the samba: The real Carioca has the samba bug under his skin and knows instinctively how to **sambar** [some 'bah] (dance the samba). If when hearing samba music or a **batucada** you feel your legs wanting to dance, but you don't know how, don't despair. It is very simple to learn how to dance the samba. It's just a matter of shaking your body and moving your feet in the following fashion:

Count one, two, three, four to the beat. While lifting your right arm, take a step forward with your right foot over your left foot. Now take a step over to the left with your left foot, bringing your left arm up and around as your right foot takes a back step followed by the respective motion with the right arm. Are you still in the rhythm? Good. Complete the cycle by bringing your left foot back over the right foot, taking a step forward to the right, thus beginning a new cycle to the beat.

It's simple. Just keep those hips moving!

Now that you have the basic samba down, you might want to try the real samba. Just follow the footsteps below, and you'll be **sambando** [some 'bun doo] (doing the samba) like a true Carioca in no time.

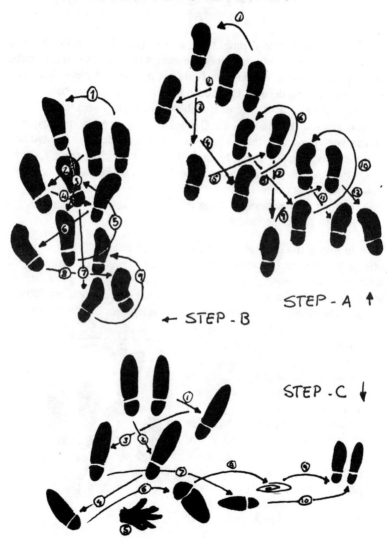

STEP - A ↑

← STEP - B

STEP - C ↓

The samba is a very energetic dance with a rhythm which induces the dancer to shout specific samba words of joy. While dancing, the following should be shouted frequently in order to enhance the feeling of the samba:

- **ô skindô skindô** [oh shkeen 'doh shkeen 'doh]
- **ziriguidum ziriguidum** [zee ree gee 'doon zee ree gee 'doon]

Obs.: These words have absolutely no meaning, but they do create a great beat.

What to wear: Anything, or close to nothing, is appropriate to wear when doing the samba. But if you're a closet queen who has always dreamt of venturing out in public wearing lace and high heels, now is your chance. All your fantasies are acceptable and encouraged. The Carioca woman seems to have a preference for baby dolls and garter belts. Don't ask why. So boys and girls, just dig into that lingerie drawer, and you will fit right in.

Where to do the samba: Anywhere there is a **batucada** is a fine place to dance the samba.

The holiday: Cariocas love Carnaval, primarily since it is a potential ten-day vacation. The holiday itself is officially on Carnaval Tuesday and Ash Wednesday until noon, when the work schedules are supposed to resume. But forget that! Since the Carioca will begin his Carnaval festivities a month *before* Carnaval, when the actual event comes around he is so "partied out" he will often take advantage of the holiday to leave town. This pilgrimage will begin on the Thursday night preceding Carnaval in order to avoid the Friday traffic. No one is *really* expected to show up at the office on Ash Wednesday at noon, and on the Thursday and Friday after Carnaval nothing *really* happens. Therefore, the Carioca will return to town on the following Monday at noon in order to avoid the Sunday night traffic.

Those diehards who have a passion for the samba school parades and participate by joining a school or two every year will return to Rio specifically for that event, then quickly go back to their vacation spots after their night of glory is over. This leaves Rio free game for the Carnaval-loving Cariocas, the tourists, and those of dubious sexual preference.

Ziriguidum!

Lesson 12

The Carioca Winter

Winter in Rio lasts for a week. A bad winter will last for two.

What to wear: When the street thermometers register 18°C (65°F) you will finally have that long-awaited opportunity to wear all those sweaters, jackets, and boots you bought in Buenos Aires before arriving in Rio. Wear them all at the same time, and you will fit right in. A Carioca would.

What to do: See Lesson 10, "The Carioca Summer."

Health Problems,
Carioca Style

The true Carioca believes he is never alone and that all aspects of his life are governed by spirits, both good and evil. Although predominantly a Catholic country, the Carioca will not hesitate to call upon any number of these spirits for comfort or healing.

If you should find yourself ill or in need while visiting Rio, do as the Carioca does. Before calling the nearest doctor, go to your local newsstand and pick up a guide to **simpatia** [seen pah 'tchee yah], a healing ritual always preceded by a prayer to a favorite spiritual guide (a guardian angel, patron saint, or guru).

In order to receive full benefits through **simpatia**, it is important to note the following guidelines before commencing down the road to well-being:

1. The objective of your **simpatia** should be honest and not prejudice anyone or anything.
2. Love conquered through occult healing forces will not last forever—between three to seven years.
3. Never attempt a **simpatia** within twenty-four hours of sexual intercourse.
4. Abstain from alcohol and sex for seven days after exercising any form of **simpatia**.
5. No **simpatia** should be practiced during the waning moon.
6. Never permit the presence of children or pregnant women when performing a **simpatia**.

Adhering to these few simple rules, the next step is to simply look up your particular malady in your **simpatia** guidebook and carefully follow the instructions. After all, it can't hurt, it's free, and it will probably take your mind off whatever it is that is bothering you. The following are a few examples of common physical, emotional, or mental ailments you, too, might possibly cure by turning to **simpatia**.

To remove warts: At night, take a piece of slab bacon to an ant hill. Rub the bacon over your wart three times while saying, **"Disaparece, veruga"** [dee zah pah 'rreh see veh 'hoo gah] ("Disappear, wart"). Put the bacon inside the ant hill and leave without looking back. Soon your wart will disappear.

To cure baldness: Clip hair from your armpits, placing the hair in a glass. Add one spoon of honey and two of Coca-Cola (Pepsi will do) and mix it together into a paste. Light two candles by the glass and let it sit overnight. *Note:* If one of the candles goes out during the night, this **simpatia** will not work. The next night, rub the mixture in the glass on your head, leaving it on for two hours. Your hair should begin to grow on the full moon of the third month after your application.

To cure a pimple inside the nose: If a pimple should develop inside your nose, gently run your fingers on the outside of the area where the pimple is developing. Heat a small white rag by holding it against a pot of boiling beans. Wring out the rag and twist it in such a way as to insert it in the nostril. Leave it on the pimple for a minute and remove. Heat the rag and repeat the process three times.

To cure allergies: Make cotton balls equalling the number of birthdays you have celebrated. Put the cotton balls in a metal container, wet them with alcohol, and light them. When the flames have extinguished, inhale the smoke, immediately collect the ashes which have remained in the container, throw them into running water, and carefully wash your hands and the container. (Be sure to place the lid on the alcohol and remove it from the area before lighting the fire.)

Simpatia is a handy cure for *all* that might ail you. To protect a home from jealousy, to find a lover for a widow, to never lack for money are just a few of the reasons a Carioca will turn to **simpatia**. The following are examples of problems you, too, might have, but never knew how to solve:

To marry a rich man: Gather three shells from the sea, three strands of your hair, three pieces of red ribbon, and three cloves of garlic. Wrap them together in a piece of white cloth. Go to the sea and throw it in the waves while focusing your thoughts on that rich man you've had your eye on (but who doesn't know you exist).

To receive long-awaited money: Locate a frog's home and check to see if the animal is in there. If it is, cover the hole and say, "I will only open your home when I receive the money that I am waiting for." When the money is received, free the frog. It is important you remember to do this since, if you don't, it is certain that you will have seven years of bad luck.

To quit drinking: Place seventy-two grains of corn inside a bottle of red wine. Leave it in the cupboard for seven nights. Whenever you feel the desire to drink, open the bottle and smell the liquid for thirty seconds. Afterwards, take a deep breath, fill a wine glass with the wine, and throw it out the kitchen door.

So if you should find yourself in one of these unfortunate circumstances while visiting Rio, just tell your friends you are resorting to **simpatia,** and your status as a Carioca will be intact. Of course, if your problem requires more immediate care, Rio has several excellent municipal hospitals completely staffed for any emergency. (See Lesson 19, "Famous Carioca Lines.")

Lesson 14

Uh, Oh...It's the Police

Being a Carioca you will inevitably find yourself in a situation in which contact with the **polícia** is required. Whether it be a traffic problem, an encounter with a **pivete**, or a robbery in your home, you can feel safe knowing that Rio's finest, those brave Cariocas who make a living upholding the law, are always ready to come to your assistance.

For example, if you have been held up and have been relieved of your new tennis shoes and your watch, simply locate the nearest police booth (conveniently located on many street corners), and report the incident. The police officer will then radio in to the nearest patrol car which should arrive within the hour to take your statement and investigate the occurrence.

If you hear intruders trying to break into your apartment during the night, a quick phone call to the nearest police station should result in an armed officer arriving at your door in nothing less than an hour. In the event there is no answer at the police station, or the line is busy, wait for ten or twenty minutes, and try again. (Refer to Lesson 15, "Using the Phone.") After all, the officers probably just stepped away from their desks for a **cafezinho** break. If they are just on a break, someone will eventually answer to take your complaint, and a **camburão** (paddy wagon) will be on its way.

WHEN YOU ARE IN THE WRONG

Often, due to uncontrollable circumstances, even the most conscientious Carioca on wheels might find himself with an expired driver's license (or no license at all), invalidated car registration papers, an inoperable fire extinguisher, or no seat belts or mandatory liability insurance. If when driving your car you are pulled over by a police officer in a routine blitz, or **dura** ['doo rrah], and all is not in order, you are in luck! Carioca police officers tend to be extremely accommodating, and they will do whatever they can to get you back on the road with the minimum of inconvenience. Due to this obliging disposition and your being a Carioca, when finding yourself on the wrong end of the stick you'll have the opportunity to resort to the common **jeitinho** in order to quickly resolve this potentially bothersome dilemma.

How to apply the jeitinho: In order to successfully apply the **jeitinho** when pulled over by the Carioca police, first create a friendly relationship with the attending officer. Then generate a gracious atmosphere by showing your respect for his position as upholder of the law. This respect may be gained by addressing him in any one of the following manners:

- **senhor** [sen 'nyoh]: Sir
- **seu guarda** ['seyoo 'gwah dah]: Mr. Guard
- **autoridade** [oh toh ree 'dah gee]: Authority

Obs.: Never address a police officer as **caninha** (cop). If you do, all chances of "resolving" your situation will be ruined.

Next, to determine whether the officer is willing to help you settle the affair amiably and with as little inconvenience as possible, simply proceed in the following manner:

Step 1. When the police officer approaches your car window, give him a thumbs-up, then say:
  "E aí, seu guarda? Tá numa boa?"
  ("So what's up, Mr. Guard? Everything OK?")
Step 2. If the issue at hand, for example, is an expired driver's license, pull out your expired one and smile, saying:
  "Aí, o negócio é o seguinte..."

Don't forget. Your explanation should be dramatic, taking no less than four minutes.

Step 3. If the officer doesn't seem to be buying your story, and you still haven't received the desired response, put on an innocent face and say:

"Seu guarda, num dá pra dá um jeitinho?"
("Mr. Guard, isn't there a way around this?")

NUM DÁ PRA DÁ UM JEITINHO?...

Of course, you may not get out of that ticket and paying that fine, but it is worth the try! And remember: since it is second nature, a true Carioca will always try the **jeitinho**.

When it's time to grease the palm: It is at this point that a true Carioca will instinctively appeal to the generous nature of many Carioca officers by suggesting an agreement—along the lines of "You scratch my back and I'll scratch yours." In other words, the officer won't have to fill out that tiresome paper work, and you won't have to suffer any further inconveniences or delays. It's been said that on occasion the officer himself might generously ask the motorist, "Do you want a **multa** (fine)?" In this case you are bound to have a clear shot at applying the **jeitinho**.

Whatever the circumstances, being a Carioca, offer half, insisting it is all you have. If agreed upon, friendly smiles will be exchanged, he will bid you a **boa viagem** (good trip), and you will be back on the road **rapidinho** (quickly) but not before receiving his kindly advice not to do whatever you did again. If you are on the highway, you may even receive a tip from your new friend, the police officer, on how to avoid the next police **dura** which is waiting for you a few kilometers down the road.

A FEW IMPORTANT TIPS

In an effort to protect innocent citizens from undesirable elements, Carioca police tend to be heavily armed. Therefore, it is important to heed the following recommendations whenever summoned by local authorities while on the road:

1. Always stop. If you don't, you might find your car, or yourself, furnished with new air-conditioning vents. If you survive, the odds of developing a friendly relationship with the policeman, in this case, will be extremely poor.

2. Always smile and remain calm. By irritating the officer you might be taken to the police station where the **jeitinho** is more complex and more difficult to negotiate. Meeting the **delegado** (sheriff) could put a big dent in your style.

3. Do not let the officers impound your car. Since they will probably figure it is stolen—therefore free game—you stand a good chance of eventually recovering it free of hubcaps, radio, and tire jack—but complete with a new set of shiny smooth tires.

4. Don't be fooled by the local patrol cars, those rusty **camburas** with the bald tires. Even though there is a Carioca behind the wheel, they will never catch up to you—but you can be sure that the machine gun bullets will!

Lesson 15

Using the Phone

Contrary to what you may have heard previously, Brazil's telephone service is right up there with the First World's. You can dial directly to most parts of Brazil and the world, international operators speak English, there is an information service (sort of), there exist telephone books (1988), public telephones are plentiful, and you can call ship to shore. Even cellular phones are now available.

So you might be asking yourself, "Why is there a lesson on using the telephone if the system is so great?" If you were a Carioca you wouldn't ask that question. Since using the phone in Rio is often an adventure, check out the following **jeitinhos.** They might be useful the next time you decide to let your finger do the walking.

Getting a dial tone: If you pick up the phone and you don't hear a hum, your phone is dead. Go the nearest public phone, call the telephone company, and report it. (They'll promise to fix it within forty-eight hours, and you can rest assured it will be fixed ON the forty-eighth hour.) If you do get a hum, though, but no dial tone, wait a few seconds, hang up the phone, then quickly pick it up. If you still don't hear a dial tone, hit the hang-up button several times, hang up, and try again. If you are *still* unsuccessful, you may be forced to resort to the following measures:

1. Shake the phone vigorously and stretch out the telephone cord;
2. Leave it off the hook while you take a bath or shower;
3. Ask your phone nicely to please allow you to make a call;
4. Dial 821-348-149-460346. This number goes nowhere, but it might make you feel better;
5. Slam down the phone using the appropriate language, and go to a public phone.

Dialing a Carioca phone: If it's your lucky day and you have managed to get a dial tone, your next step will be to dial your number.

Never dial all the numbers in immediate sequence. Either the line will go busy after the first few numbers, or it will just remain toneless. The correct Carioca procedure for dialing a phone is the following:

Step 1. Dial the first three numbers, pause for a few seconds, then dial the remaining numbers.

Step 2. Try dialing veeeery slowly, pausing between each number. If you get a busy signal immediately, it's a sure sign the call hasn't gone through.

Step 3. If the number you want is 274-5678, for example, try dialing 1+1 8-1 2+2 6-1 3+3 8-1 7+1. The phone might add and subtract itself, and you'll reach the desired number.

Step 4. Try dialing a wrong number just to test the phone.

Step 5. Slam down the receiver, pause for a moment to compose yourself, and repeat Step 1 several more times.

Step 6. Slam the phone on the floor uttering the appropriate language, and go to a public phone.

If you get a wrong number: You have gotten a dial tone, the number you dialed is finally ringing, and—hallelulia!—someone is answering. The conversation could go something like this:

—**Alô! É 234-5671?** (Hello. Is this 234-5671?)
—**Não. É 543-8910.** (No. It's 543-8910.)
—**Uééé... Como é que pode?** (Hmmm... How can that be?)
—**Bom, aqui é 543-8910. Tenta discar 309-3239, que é a subtração do seu número do meu.** (Well, this is 543-8910. Try dialing 309-3239 which is the remainder of our two phone numbers.)
—**Pô aí, valeu.** (Thanks.)

It's enough to make you wonder if your fingers have a life of their own. Anyway, if you should reach the same number three times in a row, do as the Carioca does: ask the "wrong number" to kindly leave his phone off the hook for a few minutes, which should allow you the opportunity to reach other wrong numbers. By the fifth try, if you are still reaching wrong numbers, slam the phone on the floor, and go to a public phone. A Carioca would.

Making "Economy Calls": Once you have managed to complete your call to the correct party and are deep in conversation, you might find you have been selected for one of the phone company's special services, the free-of-charge "Economy Call." Recognizing that their services are a bit steep and that others might be wanting to use the line, the phone company will be kind enough to automatically cut you off mid-sentence. If your call becomes an "Economy Call," hang up the phone and wait for the other person to return your call. When asked why you didn't call them back, just say you couldn't get a dial tone, and they will understand. This is a sure way of reducing those nasty end-of-the-month bills. Of course, for obvious reasons, a true Carioca will not be shy in selecting himself for an "Economy Call."

Special effects: Another free-of-charge courtesy of the local phone company, the Carioca telephone comes equipped with strange voices, electronic sounds, and other special effects. To enjoy this special service simply dial a number, get to a crucial point in your conversation, and the special effects will be activated.

Tuning in to "Conference Calls": If you have a need to make a conference call while in Rio, pick up the receiver, wait for your dial tone, and place your call. Within seconds you will be joined on the line by a third, or even a fourth, party. The Carioca "Conference Call" will often turn into a name-calling, shouting match between all parties involved. As a matter of principle, a real Carioca will never hang up before the other parties on the line.

Carioca telephone body language: A Carioca will always carry on telephone conversations in a standing position, thus avoiding broken **cafezinho** cups, tipped over water glasses, or smashed lamps. Even though the person on the other end of the line can't see you, just keep those hands flying and you, too, will be carrying on a phone conversation like a Carioca.

Beijinhos, tchau tchau (little kisses, bye bye): Don't think those kisses and hugs are dispensed of while on the phone. Even if you can't make that all important physical contact, it is imperative you send it over the wires. There are only two acceptable forms in which to terminate any phone conversation with another Carioca, and neither one is "good-bye." Use either the more formal or the more intimate version, and you will be signing off like a real Carioca.

 "**Um beijo**" [oon 'bay joo]: "A kiss" (casually intimate) or "**Um abraço**" [oon ah 'brrah soo]: "A hug" (more formal); correct response for both: "**Outro**" ['oh trroo]: "Another"

Using a Carioca public phone: If you should find yourself needing to make a quick phone call while away from home, you will find an **orelhão** [oh rre 'lyown] (public phone) conveniently located on many of the city's busiest street corners. When using it, proceed in the following manner:

Step 1. Look for a large yellow, ear-shaped object. If you're lucky there will be a red phone inside it. This is the public phone, or **orelhão** (meaning "big ear"), as the locals affectionately refer to it. (Sometimes you may come across blue phones; these are reserved for making collect calls.)

Step 2. Buy a **ficha** ['fee shah] (token). No need to dig into your pocket for some coins here. **Orelhões** live on **fichas** which can be purchased at most newsstands. Note that the times you need to use a public phone will coincide with the times that you are out of **fichas** which, for some reason, tend to be in the middle of the night when a newsstand is not handy or they are all closed. A true Carioca will always carry a few **fichas**.

Step 3. Wait in line. In the time it took for you to go to a newsstand, buy the fichas, and get back, a line of people needing to use the service will have formed.

Step 4. When it is your turn, insert a **ficha** in the appropriate slot, and dial your number. Hopefully, the intended party will answer, at which time you should firmly insert one finger in your ear, hold the mouthpiece to your lips, and shout your message as quickly as possible.

Step 5. After a few moments you will hear a click, and the line will go dead. Don't put down the receiver. If you do, the person behind you will think you have terminated your call, will demand his turn, and you will be required to repeat Step 3.

Step 6. Repeat Step 4.

WHAT YOU *WON'T* HEAR ON A CARIOCA ORELHÃO

"Please deposit 75 centavos for the first three minutes Sir."
"If you want to stay on the line, please deposit 25 centavos
for the next three minutes."
"Please find your change in the appropriate slot."
"Thank you for using TELERJ. Have a nice day."

Lesson 16

Carioca Romance

If you are taking a vacation for romance, you have come to the right place. Cariocas are very high on the World's Most Romantic People list, and the promise of romance is in their music, the way they talk, and the rhythm of their walk. Go ahead. Loosen up that stride and practice your body language. You never know, you could meet that special someone right here in Rio.

How to get a date in Rio: Single, married, young, or old, it is second nature for the Carioca to always be on the lookout. Making contact with a new person specifically for romantic purposes is a personal challenge the Carioca meets with great enthusiasm, creativity, and guts. When the opportunity presents itself it takes precedence over all. Consider the following scenario, for example:

You are late for an important business meeting and are stuck sitting in your car while stopped at a traffic light. The cross traffic is intense, making it impossible to run the light. You can either stare straight ahead and stew about the time you are wasting, or you can

do as the Carioca does: In first gear, keep one foot on the clutch while the other accelerates. Check out all the cars around you for an interesting **gata.** If you see one, honk your horn a few times in an attempt to make eye contact, and when the light changes, squeeze in behind her and flick your high beams (at least five times). If you are lucky, you will be exchanging phone numbers at the next stop light!

Of course, you could take a lesson from one particular Carioca gentleman who met two of his wives by provoking "fender-benders." He insists that the satisfaction of meeting these women far outweighed the damages to his car.

No need for women to be left out in the cold either. One certain well-known woman, noticing a **gato** walking his dog on the sidewalk in front of her building every day, ran out and bought a similar dog. The next day she simply stopped the **gato** on the sidewalk, suggested their dogs meet, and it was the beginning of a beautiful relationship.

So get out there, be seductive, and take a look. Opportunity is probably knocking right under your nose.

Setting up the Carioca date: Rio offers many sophisticated restaurants and night clubs where you can drop a wad of bills and impress that special someone. On the other hand, by romancing Carioca style, your wallet will suffer less, and your new status as a Carioca will remain intact. The following is a suggestion for that special night out on the town:

1. Arrange to pick up your date at 8:30 p.m.
2. Call her at 8:45 p.m. to verify that the date is still on.
3. Arrive at her building at 9:30 p.m. and take the elevator up to her apartment. Upon entering her front door, be sure to kiss her mother, her aunts, her sisters, and her grandmothers on both cheeks and to shake hands with her father, her brothers, her uncles, and her grandfathers. Don't forget to make contact with the maid, as she will ultimately have the final word on whether you are **simpático** (nice) or not.
4. Accept a **cafezinho,** then spend at least thirty minutes **fazendo sala** (making small talk) with her family. Acceptable topics for conversation are the weather (too hot), crime (the **pivete** who took off with your tennis shoes), inflation (blame it on the First World), and the latest episode of the **novela das oito**.

5. When the conversation gets slow, or the ten o'clock program begins on television, take your leave by kissing all the women on both cheeks, shaking the men's hands, and stopping by the kitchen to compliment the maid on her excellent **cafezinho** before heading for the elevator.

6. Drive around **baixo** (lower) Leblon and Gavea, the areas with the greatest concentration of **barzinhos**, passing at least three times by each place to check out the crowd.

7. Settle at your favorite **barzinho** and order a portion of french fries and a couple of **chopps** or **caipirinhas**. Be sure to sit next to each other and not across from each other. In this position you will be able to appreciate the action and comment on everyone else, thus ensuring a constant flow of conversation (and avoiding those uncomfortable silences).

8. If by now all is going well and you want to spend some private time together, the true Carioca will take his date to:

- the back seat of his car by a trailer on Barra beach,
- the back seat of his car by the parking lot at Joatinga beach, or
- a special suite at a motel.

Motels: If you think that motels are for families on the road or the drowsy traveler, guess again. Motels are for SEX..Due to the Cariocas' crowded living conditions, the only place where you can really be alone *and* comfortable is a motel, and Rio has hundreds to choose from. Get a special suite so you can have the option of enjoying the indoor and outdoor pools, the sauna, the hot tub, and a full course meal if the going gets slow. Even Cariocas aren't made of steel!

Don't worry about stopping at a pharmacy before heading for the motel. Brazil's **Lei da Camisinha** ("Little Shirt" or Prophylactic Law) makes it mandatory for all motels to distribute the necessary protection at the motel's reception gate.

Privacy isn't a problem either. Closed garages hide your license plate and hidden side entrances guarantee uninterrupted service. No need to rush off to Barra (where you'll find the largest concentration of motels in the **Zona Sul**) if you should get the urge while at the office during lunchtime. **Centro** (downtown) offers a vertical motel where, in lieu of garages, your privacy is assured by the masks which are issued when registering in order to avoid those embarrassing and untimely encounters.

Saying good night: When it comes time to say good night, remember that Cariocas love to be romantic. It isn't by chance that Vinicius de Moraes and Tom Jobim are Cariocas. So if while on your date you hear bells and your heart skips a beat, don't be shy. Call her **gatinha**, tell her that she is the most gorgeous creature this side of heaven, and then set up that all important next date before kissing her good night. If your date turns out to be a **baranga**, tell her that she is the most gorgeous creature this side of heaven, and then kiss her good night saying:

 "**Te ligo. A gente se vê.**" [tchee 'lee goo ah 'gen tche see'veh]: "I'll call you. See you around."

A real Carioca NEVER passes up a challenge to seduce.

Staying in: If it's the end of the month and the Carioca is feeling the pinch on his wallet, staying in and watching the tube with his date is always an option. But if you plan to stay in like a Carioca, it is essential you get

informed by tuning in to the eight o'clock news program before pushing
that tape into the video cassette. The daily news topics will include:

- how to calculate the minimum wage,
- the government corruption scandal of the day,
- the most recent bank robbery,
- the price increases of the day,
- the new coach for the national soccer team,
- the current Formula One news, and
- the weather, which will be
  > sunny and clear to partially cloudy;
  > subject to rain (but maybe not).

Don't put in that tape yet! Following the news comes the backbone of
national television, the **novela das oito.** The stars of these prime time soap
operas are national idols, and a true Carioca will go to great lengths not to
miss a single episode. Imagine a soap opera starring Marlon Brando and
Madonna, and you might get the picture.

Consequently, every night of the week, with the exception of Sundays,
a real Carioca will *never* do the following between 8:30 and 9:30 p.m.:

- schedule a date
- make a phone call
- eat dinner
- entertain

- go to the local store for milk
- fill the car's tank at the gas station
- drop in on someone
- feed the family pet

Note: The only exception to this rule is when the hour-long show,
affectionately referred to as **Quem Rouba Mais** *(Who Steals More),* is aired
simultaneously on every television station directly following the news. For
months prior to elections, this enlightening program is generously spon-
sored by the various national political parties: namely the PT, PTR, PDB,
PMDB, PFDB, PC, PDS, PFL, PRN, PV, etc.

NOW is the time for that tape.

And remember, before saying good night to your date, be sure to make
the appropriate body contact with ALL of her relatives who have been
sitting in front of the tube with you.

Lesson 17

The Carioca Child

Being a Carioca is a state of mind that knows no age boundaries. Therefore, if you are a parent, it is important that your offspring follow in your footsteps down the road to becoming a true Carioca.

ESSENTIAL PHRASES

The following phrases are the heart of the Carioca child's vocabulary, all of which may be directed at the nursemaid, maid, mother, father, grandmother, aunt, or any other able being who happens to be in the vicinity.

As a matter of fact, some Carioca children will even continue to successfully use these phrases well into adulthood:

Eu quero [ayoo 'keeeeeeeeeeeh rroo]: I want. (As in *"Eu quero um sorvete."*: "I want an ice cream.")

Me dá [meeeeeee 'daaaaaaaaaaahh]: Give me.

Num quero [noom 'keeeeeeeeh rroo]: I don't want. (As in *"Num quero legumes."*: "I don't want any vegetables.")

Num fui eu [noom 'foy ayoo]: It wasn't me.

For maximum effectiveness when using any one of these phrases, your Carioca child should:

A. repeat it at least five times,

B. shout it in the loudest voice possible,

C. never interrupt whatever it is he is doing when using it, and

D. direct the phrase to everyone and anyone (preferably family members and maids).

WHAT TO FEED YOUR CARIOCA CHILD

Since Carioca children are NOT very fond of variety when it comes to food, they are very easy to feed. To avoid any problems, though, while at home or at a restaurant, only nourish your Carioca child with the following:

- **bife** ['bee fee]: a thin steak
- **batata frita** [bah tah tah 'frree tah]: french fries
- **arroz e feijão** [ah'hoiz ee fey 'jown]: rice and beans
- **macarrão** [mah kah 'hown]: noodles

Obs.:It is imperative that you never place anything else, especially if it's green, on or near your Carioca child's plate. And unless your child is drinking a soft drink, be sure to put at least three heaping tablespoons of sugar in the glass before serving it—and that includes milk.

MUTUAL EXPECTATIONS

Naturally, as a Carioca parent you will expect a lot from your offspring. You will expect your child to study hard, get good grades, have nice friends, come home early, and not get involved with people of dubious character. But a few things you should *never* expect your Carioca child to do are:

A. work as a cashier or in the kitchen at Bob's during summer vacation,
B. do volunteer work at a child care center after school,
C. work serving tables to earn money to buy a car, or
D. do any housework.

In return, your child will want:

A. a **mesada** (allowance),
B. a trip to Disney World,
C. a car when he turns sixteen, and
D. presents on Children's Day (October 12).

PÔ, AÍ...
VÔ MANDÁ VÊ
NO SKATE !

AFTER SCHOOL HOURS A CARIOCA CHILD WILL

Demand lunch.

Go to the beach.

Have lessons in English or French at the local language school.

Take Judo lessons at the nearest academy.

Have ballet lessons in Copacabana.

Swim laps with the local athletic club's swimming team.

Play **futebol de botão** (button soccer) with the other **pirralhos** (noisy, irritating little ones) in his apartment building's game room.

Watch dubbed Japanese adventure programs or the afternoon **novela** (soap opera) reruns on television.

AFTER SCHOOL HOURS A CARIOCA CHILD *WON'T*

Stay after school for cheerleading or sports team practice.

Have a part time job at the local ice cream parlor.

Earn allowance money by raking the leaves in the back yard.

Baby-sit the neighbor's kids to save enough for new clothes.

Go home to clean up his or her room.

Help out Mom by washing or drying dishes.

Do any laundry.

Wash or wax the car.

Study.

Lesson 18

Gambling —
Legal and Not So Legal

If you have the urge to gamble while in Rio, you are in luck. Although the government outlawed casinos in the early fifties, many gambling options—legal and not so legal—are available, and the true Carioca will earmark a healthy portion of his monthly paycheck to try his luck at one or all of them.

Jogo do Bicho (Animal Game): Other than traffic violations, the **Jogo do Bicho** numbers racket is probably the most tolerated illegal activity in Rio. On just about every street corner in Rio you will come across a group of

people milling around an individual sitting on a crate behind a small wooden desk, selling what appear to be little pieces of paper with numbers on them. These numbers correspond to animals—there are some twenty-one animals to choose from. To bet just choose the animal that appeared in your dreams the night before. Once a day the winning number will be announced over the radio, and if you are the lucky winner, you might receive about twenty-to-one on your initial investment.

The **Jogo do Bicho** began in the late 1800's as a means of generating funds for a wealthy baron's private zoo. Whoever visited the zoo was given a piece of paper with the drawing of an animal on it. At the end of the day a flag depicting the winning animal was flown over the zoo, and the winners would take home prize money. Once the zoo managed to collect the funds they needed the game was canceled, although its popularity flourished.

Today, **bicheiros**, or owners of the **Jogo do Bicho**, are some of the wealthiest and most powerful people in Rio. And even though it is illegal, it still thrives, supposedly collecting funds to support the various samba schools in the yearly Carnaval parade. Don't worry though. That man in front of you in the betting line is probably the local cop placing his bet, too. So the next time you dream of a lion or a dog, run—don't walk—to the nearest corner, and place your bets.

Loteria Federal: Just sit at a sidewalk café, or stop at a street light, and you will be approached by a scruffy looking character selling colorful sheets of tickets with numbers on them. Buy one or several of these tickets, and you will be in the running for big-time money, courtesy of the Brazilian government. If a Carioca sees a number which corresponds to his telephone, license plate, birthday, identification, or social security number, he will spend at least a week's salary on **Loteria** (loh teh 'rree yah) tickets and call it a good investment.

Loteria Esportiva (Loteca): Regardless what those **Paulistas**, **Mineiros**, and **Gaúchos** might say, Rio is the soccer mecca of Brazil. What, with Maracanã Stadium and the local Flamengo, Botafogo, and Fluminense teams, who could possibly dispute that? By filling out a little card at his corner betting house once a week, the Carioca has the chance to pick the winner (or tie) of fourteen different soccer matches and win zillions of cruzeiros. Also called **Certo ou Errado** (Right or Wrong), this is one game you can win by losing. Miss guessing the outcome of *all* the games and you will be in the money. It's almost as much fun as playing the real thing, and you don't run the risk of walking around with a cast on your foot for a month.

The Loto and the Sena: Purchased at your local betting house, these two games differ only in the amount of numbers you can play on each betting card. The Carioca's favorites, winnings are also in the zillions, depending on how many numbers you guessed correctly on each card.

Raspadinhas: The baby of legal gambling, these "little shaved ones" resemble those popular Scratch and Sniffs. Just buy a card and scratch off the coating on the designated areas to see if you are an instant winner. In this case, there isn't a lot to win, but the gratification is immediate.

Video poker and clandestine casinos: Definitely illegal and clearly frowned upon by the authorities, no Carioca in his right mind would be caught involved in either one of these forms of gambling unless, of course, he is a **bicheiro,** or the offspring of one.

Famous Carioca Lines

Although waiting in line is a national pastime, the Carioca considers it a happening and affectionately refers to line waiting as a **programa de índio**—meaning what Indians do for entertainment. Seeing a line forming anywhere, the Carioca will figure there must be something interesting at the end of it and will simply take his place in line. In fact, recent studies have shown that Cariocas spend more than thirty percent of their time patiently waiting in lines. Really...

In the event you find yourself face to face with a Carioca line, do as the Carioca does. Resort to any one of the following common **jeitinhos**, and it won't be *that* bad after all:

1. Send your office boy to wait for you;
2. Solicit a street urchin to wait for you;
3. Find someone you know near the front of the line to get for you whatever it is everyone is waiting for;
4. Hire someone to get for you whatever it is everyone is waiting for;
5. Cut in line and ignore the protests (can be very dangerous);
6. Get in line, then ask the person in front of you to save your place. Go for a few **chopps** or **cafezinhos** at the **boteco**, and then return to your place in line.

The beauty of the Carioca is his ability to make the best of any situation, and line waiting is one of them. Finding himself in front of a forty to fifty minute line, the Carioca's first reaction might be to mutter, "**Tôfu**" [toh 'foo] ("I'm screwed"). But once in line he'll have a grand time making new friends and comparing opinions on current events with those sharing the same line.

Wait in a few of the following Carioca favorite lines, and soon you, too, will be feeling like a real Carioca:

- Bank line between the first and the tenth of each month
- Cash register lines at any Barra supermarket on Saturdays
- Carnaval parade ticket line
- Movie line on opening day of a major feature
- Movie line on the following week for the same movie
- La Mole restaurant line on a Saturday afternoon
- Post office line at any time of the day
- Motel car lines on a Friday night
- Duty Free Shop line at Galeão International Airport
- Customs line at Galeão International Airport
- Beverage bar line at half time during a game at Maracanã Stadium
- Gas station car lines just before any fuel price increase
- Gas station line during an alcohol shortage
- Meat market line during a meat shortage
- Poultry store line after a chicken or egg shortage
- Rest room line at the Carnaval parade
- Bus line at the downtown garage building at six p.m.
- Parking line at the São Conrado Fashion Mall on Friday nights
- Visa line at the American Consulate
- **Casa lotérica** (betting house) line on a Thursday night
- Taxi line at Santos Dumont airport at seven p.m.
- Emergency section line at any of the local municipal hospitals
- Line to get into Maracanã Stadium for a final championship game
- Line to vote on election day
- Line to receive I.N.P.S. (social security) compensations
- Line for the ten-cent-tray lunch at the state university cafeteria

Lesson 20

A Day at Maracanã

Every Carioca has a favorite **futebol** [foo tchee 'bol] (soccer) team. If you are a real Carioca, your team will be either Flamengo, Botafogo, or Fluminense, and depending which one you choose, you will be eternally referred to as a **Flamenguista, Botafoguense,** or **Tricolor** [trree coh 'loh], meaning respectively a Flamengo, Botafogo, or Fluminense fan. You will cherish your team second only to your mother and be more faithful to your team than to your own spouse. Consequently, once you have chosen your team you will despise the other two for as long as you live. If a team other than yours is playing a team from São Paulo, for example, in the finals of a national championship, you will simply ignore the entire event. Under all circumstances, a true Carioca will *only* acknowledge the existence of his own team.

A Carioca, come flood or famine, will never miss seeing his team play at Maracanã, the world's largest stadium. Although it was a team from São Paulo who, by some fluke, won the inaugural game in 1950, the first goal was scored by a Carioca, thus confirming Cariocan supremacy on the field.

GOING TO MARACANÃ

Before leaving for the stadium, meet your **galera do futebol** (your group of friends who are also soccer fans) at a **boteco** for a few **choppinhos**. Be sure that everyone is wearing a team shirt, and don't forget your **radinho** [ha 'gee nyoo] (the cheapest radio available) and some sort of drum substitute, if not the real thing.

Whether taking the bus or driving (take the car least likely to be stolen), be sure to intimidate any rival fans along the way by waving flags, shirts, or banners out the window while chanting your team's name. If you are a **Flamenguista**, for example, chant:

☞   **"Meeeeeen-goooooo, Meeeeeen-goooooo"**
["Maaaaaayn-gooooooow, Maaaaaaayn-gooooooow"]

Make your way through the traffic and the crowds to the stadium. If you boast of a stomach lined with lead, stop at one of the "foot-long hot dog" stands before entering the stadium gate. And don't forget the onion and tomato sauce!

Once inside the stadium, a real Carioca **futebol** fan will only sit in the **arquibancada** (bleachers) where chaos is at its maximum. Having located a place to sit and are settled, be sure to behave in the following fashion (a real Carioca **futebol** fan would):

1. Start a **batucada** by banging on your drums or on the seats surrounding your seat;
2. Drink **chopps** from the mobile vendors;
3. Demoralize the referee's mother and the rest of his family;
4. Bounce your smashed **chopp** paper cup, as hard as you can, off the head of the person seated in front of you; then pretend it came from the seats behind yours;
5. Continuously chant your team's name.

Obs.: Beware of cups filled with bodily fluids projected from the seats directly above yours.

Acceptable conduct during the game: If your team should score a goal, work yourself into a frenzy by jumping and screaming, and then hug the stranger jumping up and down next to you. Maintain this euphoria for a minimum of five minutes. Next, continue to give your team incentive throughout the game by conducting yourself in the rowdiest manner possible.

In the unfortunate event the opposing team should score a goal against your team, your entire section of the **arquibancada** will fall into five minutes of stunned silence. At this point, resist the temptation to abandon the game. Simply lean over to the person seated closest to you and place the blame for your team's poor performance on the following:

     A. the current economic crisis,
     B. the current political crisis,
     C. the trading of Brazil's best players to European teams,
     D. the Church, and
     E. the **bicheiros**.

It goes without being said that the coach should be fired on the spot and then be sent to São Paulo as a trainer for one of the **Paulista** teams.

2 x 0 ['doysh ah 'zeh rroo]: In the event your team is clearly headed for disaster, take off your shirt, slip out the side door quietly in order to avoid the traffic, and take an alternative route to the nearest **boteco** for a few **chopps.** There is nothing more humiliating for a defeated Carioca **futebol** fan than to be jeered and mocked in Maracanã traffic by the triumphant fans of the winning team.

If your team is victorious, wrap yourself up in your flag, take advantage of every opportunity to jeer and mock the defeated fans, and head straight to the nearest **boteco** for a few **chopps.**

    "Meeeeeeen-gooooooo, Meeeeeeen-gooooooo!"

Holidays and the Four-Day Weekend

Granted, there are a lot of national holidays in Brazil with all the saints to honor and what not. In an effort not to short change Brazilians when it comes to their holidays, the federal government has passed many laws over the years declaring when national holidays should be celebrated. To give you an idea, the following law (verbatim) was decreed a few years back establishing the correct manner in which to observe official holidays:

> ...Holidays will be observed on the previous Monday when they fall on the other days of the week. This also applies to holidays falling on Saturdays or Sundays. If the holiday occurs on Election Day, it will not be anticipated for another day. In case there is more than one holiday in the same week, the latter will be observed on Monday of the following week. If by any chance there is already a holiday in the following week, it will be observed on Monday, while the previous holiday will be celebrated on Tuesday.

But, like many laws, they are short lived, *and* so was this one.

Regardless, Cariocas love holidays and take them very seriously. So seriously, in fact, that they feel obliged to extend them to the maximum, even when it infringes on the work week. After all, even the Carioca is entitled to determine his own personal priorities.

The following are a few of the parameters established by true Cariocas when calculating holiday time:

1. If a holiday falls on a Tuesday or a Thursday, it is automatically a four-day weekend: if it's a Thursday, it will begin at noon on the previous Wednesday, and if it's a Tuesday, it will end at noon on the following Wednesday (to accommodate for traffic problems).

2. If a holiday falls on a Wednesday, you are looking at a five-day weekend, with the potential for a nine-day weekend.

3. The end of the year holiday—beginning on Christmas Eve at noon—will last until the Monday following Easter. (Nothing *really* happens at the office between Christmas and Easter, and with the New Year's, Rio's birthday, and Carnaval holidays in between, why even make the effort to go to work?)

4. With schools closed and the children making their trips to Disney World, taking July off is completely acceptable.

Rationalizing that by showing up for work on one hundred and fifty-three days out of a possible three hundred and three he is clearly doing more than his share for the country's economy, the true Carioca considers this to be a perfectly reasonable schedule.

Note: Every four years, when Brazil plays in the World Cup Soccer Tournament, the number of required work days is directly reduced in proportion to the team's performance.

Lesson 22

No Sun? No Sweat!

Although the Carioca would rather not admit it, the sun doesn't always shine in the **Cidade Maravilhosa**. If you should find yourself in Rio on one of those rare rainy days, don't despair. The following are a just a few of the many activities that Cariocas will indulge in to pass the time until the sun breaks through, and they can get back to the beach:

1. Spend four hours at their favorite **boteco** drinking **caipirinhas** and eating a **feijoada**;
2. Spend four hours at their favorite **churrascaria** drinking **caipirinhas** and eating a **rodízio**;
3. Meet the **galera** at the **botequim** for a few **chopps** while discussing the weather;
4. Go to the movies; (see Lesson 19, "Famous Carioca Lines");
5. Stay home and watch their neighbors through telescopes or binoculars from their verandas.

Lesson 23

Your Carioca I.Q.

Are you wondering how far you've traveled down the road to becoming a really true Carioca? **Fique numa boa!** (Stay cool!) Take the following true or false quiz and test your Cariocaness:

T or F   1. Traffic in Rio flows like a dream.

T or F   2. Maracanã is a pasta dish.

T or F   3. The statue of Christ is on Sugar Loaf Mountain.

T or F   4. Cariocas never stay at the beach after five p.m.

T or F   5. Cariocas always park their cars right in front of where they're planning to go.

T or F   6. A Carioca policeman is always polite and helpful.

T or F   7. When riding on a city bus you should always hang on for dear life.

T or F   8. If you're not a local, expect a rip-off when taking a taxi.

T or F   9. Drivers in Rio are very respectful of the law and other drivers on the road.

T or F   10. There is always a place to park your car in Rio.

T or F   11. Your car is safe when there is a **flanelinha** around.

T or F   12. Someone will be leaning or sitting on your car when you return to it.

T or F   13. Your car may not be there when you return.
T or F   14. Cariocas only drink three beers.
T or F   15. Bathing suits in Rio are meant for swimming.
T or F   16. The beach is closed at night.
T or F   17. **Batucada** rhythms are made by drum playing only.
T or F   18. Cariocas love people from São Paulo.
T or F   19. A true Carioca will return home by two a.m.
T or F   20. If you're under eighteen years old, drinking at bars will be very difficult.
T or F   21. Motels in Rio are meant for tired travelers.
T or F   22. Policemen in Rio are always on the up-and-up.
T or F   23. One should not get sexually aroused while dancing the **lambada**.
T or F   24. Soccer is a Carioca sport.
T or F   25. Surfing is a Carioca sport.
T or F   26. Hang gliding is a Carioca sport.
T or F   27. Scheming is a Carioca sport.
T or F   28. Appreciating women's **bundas** is a Carioca sport.
T or F   29. A true Carioca does not need a tan.
T or F   30. The drivers triple parked in the drawing below will receive **multas**, and their cars will be towed away.

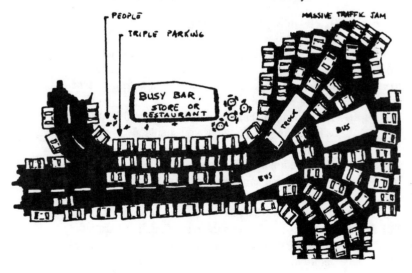

ANSWERS TO THE CARIOCA I.Q. QUIZ

1. **F.** Nightmare is more like it.
2. **F.** Maybe after the fourth **caipirinha**.
3. **F.** You must have flunked geography if you missed this one.
4. **F.** Maybe, if it's raining.
5. **T.** A parking space will be invented if there isn't one.
6. **T.** As long as you are greasing his palm.

7. **T.** And also to your purse.
8. **T.** The heavier the accent, the more expensive the ride.
9. **F.** If you answered **T**, you're in for a surprise.
10. **F.** Maybe after two a.m.
11. **F.** Your car is never safe in Rio.
12. **T.** If not trying to open it up.
13. **T.** Always carry extra money for a bus.
14. **F.** Only before the fourth one.
15. **F.** Not since the 1970's.
16. **F.** The beach is yours twenty-four hours a day!
17. **F.** A **batucada** is the use of anything available as a percussion instrument.
18. **F.** Cariocas love to make fun of them.
19. **F** Eight a.m. is more like it (in time for work).
20. **F.** Anybody who can reach the counter will be served.

21. **F.** Motels are for SEX!! If you are tired,you should go home.
22. **T.** And it snows in Rio.
23. **F.** Are you kidding?? That's the whole idea!!
24. **T.** Very much so.
25. **T.** Very much so.
26. **T.** Very much so.
27. **T.** Very much so, there is always some scheme going on.
28. **T.** Very much so, probably the most popular of all sports in Rio.
29. **F.** Yeah, right...
30. **F.** Yeah, right...

RESULTS OF THE CARIOCA I.Q. TEST

21—30 CORRECT
Aí, beleza mermão! (Hey, cool buddy!). It's time to sell the farm and move to the big city. You are definitely a true Carioca at heart.

11—20 CORRECT
You are headed on the right track. Try eating a few more day-old **coxinhas de galinha** at the **boteco**, and your score will improve, **viu**?

0—10 CORRECT
Aí! Qualé, seu gringo? (Hey! What's up, you gringo?) Pull those polyesters back out of your closet, strap on your camera, and take a taxi to Corcovado. You are indeed a tourist, pal.

Lesson 24

So You Want to Stay...

If the thought of going back to your six-digit corporate position and those payments on your house in the suburbs is making you a "bit" tense, your next step is obvious. Go ahead. Put your finger on that dial and tell your boss that you are staying in paradise, saying **"Tchau"** to your high-pressured job, and kissing that tenth-floor office (with a window) good-bye. It's time you lived like a true Carioca. The following initial steps should help you get settled in the **Cidade Maravilhosa**:

STEP 1. RENT AN APARTMENT

Your first step towards living like a Carioca will be to rent a two-bedroom apartment. (You don't want all those friends and family members who will be coming for extended visits to sleep on the floor, do you?) Be sure it has an ocean view and a veranda—so that you can appreciate the sites—and is situated no less than four blocks from the beach in the **Zona Sul**.

OCEAN VIEW

Living in a Carioca apartment you will be sharing your elevator with the other twelve apartments on your floor. Considered a bonus, sharing an elevator will offer you those optimum opportunities to meet your neighbors. Who knows? You could get in the elevator and find that special someone who, by chance, is taking his or her pet out for a walk. (Refer back to Lesson 16, "Carioca Romance.") Which reminds me, it is always wise to measure the elevator before signing that contract. You don't want to have the unpleasant surprise of finding that, when it comes time to walk your pet, you have to use the stairs. Of course, unless you want to scrimp on aerobics classes and prefer running up several flights of stairs when the electricity is cut off, it is always a good idea to consider a lower floor when choosing your apartment.

A touch of Bauhaus: No need for those nasty interior decorating bills either. Designed for efficiency, the Carioca apartment will require very little furniture—a few pillows on the floor and a fan should do fine for the living room, while a bed and chair (to stack your clothes on) in the bedrooms should do the trick. The curtain rod in the shower works beautifully for those items still lingering on in your wardrobe that might need hanging.

If by chance you are an entomologist, you will be delighted with the variety of species your apartment will be furnished with. Then again, if you're not, don't panic. It's nothing an old shoe can't take care of.

STEP 2. MEET YOUR DOORMAN

The first step you should take after renting an apartment is to develop a relationship with the **porteiro** [poh 'tay rroo] (doorman), without a doubt the most important person in the building. **Porteiros** are not Cariocas; they come from the Northeast of Brazil. If not in the garage washing cars, in one of the apartments having a **cafezinho** with a maid, or at the entrance reading someone else's newspaper, a **porteiro** can usually be found in his living quarters with his wife and three children watching television. Greet him by saying the following:

 "E aí, mermão? Beleza?":
"So hey, buddy? Everything cool?"

That way you will be guaranteed having your newspaper delivered by noon, your car "washed" daily, and your mail deposited on your doorstep at least twice a week. Also, because he is the only person who knows everyone in the building, your **porteiro** will be indispensable for:

- A. telling you if that **gata** upstairs has a boyfriend,
- B. telling you if that **gatão** downstairs has a girlfriend,
- C. letting you know that your **galera** came by while you were out,
- D. doing very minor fix-ups in your apartment,
- E. bringing the groceries up (especially if the electricity is off or the elevator is being serviced),
- F. letting the people on the floor above you know that you don't appreciate their son's drum playing at two a.m.,
- G. finding **empregadas** [eyn prreh 'gah dash] (maids) and **faxineiras** [fah shee 'nay rrash] (cleaning women),
- H. keeping your car clean, and
- I. supplying you with the best tips for the **Jogo do Bicho.**

Note: Since the salary your **porteiro** receives doesn't include the above duties, when pursuing him for any services besides sitting by the entrance to your building, a tip will be required. Simply wad up a few small bills, put them in his hand while patting him on the back, and say:

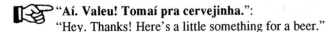 **"Aí. Valeu! Tomaí pra cervejinha."**:
"Hey. Thanks! Here's a little something for a beer."

STEP 3. HIRE A MAID

In order to free yourself for those more important items on your agenda, such as going to the beach, it is imperative that you hire an **empregada**. For a small tip, the **porteiro** is sure to come up with a relative who will be available to begin work on Monday morning at seven sharp.

How to deal with your maid: When she arrives at eleven o'clock, your first step will be to sit her down and firmly let her know exactly what you expect her to do.

It is important to keep in mind that maids will usually only do what you tell them. For example, if you request a turkey for Christmas dinner, don't be surprised if that is all you find when you and your guests sit down at the dinner table. Also, since maids often come from small towns in the interior of Brazil or the Northeast, conveniences you might take for granted are completely foreign to them. To make my point, there is the case of one **patroa** [pah 'trrow ah] (female boss) who, upon noticing there was no toilet tissue in the bathroom, asked her maid to please change it. When she went to use the facilities several hours later, the **patroa** found her maid carefully rolling tissue from the new roll to the empty one, sheet by sheet. The maid, of course, was not aware that the tissue holder was detachable from the wall!

Therefore, when dealing with your new maid, the following guidelines will help you get off on the right foot:

WHAT A CARIOCA MAID WILL DO

Demand a color television set for the kitchen.
Refuse to serve dinner after 8:30 p.m. since it would
interfere with the **novela das oito**.
Demand the month of December off to visit her
six children in the Northeast.
Ask for two nights a week off to dance at the **forró** (hick disco).
Use two kilos of sugar and one kilo of salt a week.
Leave all the lamps unplugged after cleaning behind the furniture.
Wax your antique dining room table with the floor waxer.
Go to the doctor once a week and come back only in time for dinner.
Wear your clothes and drink your booze while you are away.
Get more telephone calls than you do.

WHAT A CARIOCA MAID *WON'T* DO
Wash windows or wax floors; you will have to hire
a **faxineira** for that.
Arrive in time for breakfast on Monday morning.
Serve dinner on Fridays.
Work during Carnaval.
Remember to give you your telephone messages.
Cook anything except for rice and beans until you teach her.
Answer the phone or the front door during her **novela**.
Speak on the phone for less than fifteen minutes.

Calculating your maid's salary: Depending on her experience, you can pay anything from one minimum wage on up. It's a good idea to check with the **porteiro** first to see how much others in your building are paying so as not to inflate the market. If you pay too much, the other maids in the building will demand raises—resulting in your getting dirty looks from your neighbors in the elevator. If you pay too little, your neighbors won't hesitate to steal her away.

Once you are in agreement concerning her salary, you can simply calculate the amount to pay her each month by checking the newspaper for the current wage quotation. Then remember to watch the evening news on a daily basis in order to keep up with the latest bonus the government has conceded regarding wages. Next, either add or subtract the bonus from her salary, depending on what you paid the previous month.

By the time she has been with you for over six months you may be required to determine her salary by adding all her salaries over a six-month period, then subtracting the government stipulated bonus. If the remainder is less than what *that* month's salary is, you will have to add the bonus to her salary. If it is more, you will have to subtract in order to determine her salary for that month. Be sure to get a receipt. When it comes time, you will need to know how much you paid her previously in order to apply the most recent inflation table to your calculations. Got that?

Aside from the monthly salary, social security payments, and her bus fare, you will also be expected to fork out for:

- doctor and dental expenses when the municipal hospital lines are too long, or the doctors are on strike,
- presents for her children at Christmas time,
- extra for a down payment on her mother's television, and
- an advance for her to buy her Carnaval parade costume.

STEP 4. BUY A CAR

If you are a real Carioca, your best bet when purchasing a car is something used—at least five years old—preferably with a few dents and rust spots. That way you will avoid any nervousness on the highway or when parking, and the chances of it ending up for sale in Paraguay are "slightly" reduced.

Once you get the keys, the following recommendations may help you maximize the life expectancy of your car:

1. Always lock your steering wheel with a large padlock and turn on your alarm systems whenever you park;
2. Make sure that the *most* important item in your car, your horn, is in perfect working condition;
3. Place eight stickers on the windows and two beach chairs inside the trunk;
4. Replace your antenna with a wire coat hanger and install your sound system in the glove compartment. (Or use a walkman!)

STEP 5. PAY YOUR BILLS

Naturally, since the local currency is the cruzeiro, most of your monthly expenses, such as utilities, will be billed to you in cruzeiros. On the other hand, some debts may be billed to you in another form of currency—usually made up of several initials—which the government will have created to adjust for inflation. In order to pay *those* bills, find out how much they are worth in cruzeiros by simply making a quick call to your local bank. (Refer to Lesson 15, "Using the Phone.") And remember, since all bills must be paid at the bank or the post office (refer to Lesson 19, "Famous Carioca Lines"), be sure to take along some **trocadinho** for the **flanelinhas** who will be waiting for you.

STEP 6. GO TO THE BEACH

Your maid quit, the phones don't work, the electricity is off, your tennis shoes were stolen, and your car won't start? No problem. **Fique numa boa** (Stay cool), and do as the Carioca does. Put on a smile, slip into those **Havaianas,** and head for the sand. After all, there is nothing that a few hours at the beach won't cure. Take it from a *real* Carioca.

Falou! (All right!)

Conclusion

NOW What!

Valeu! You bought this book and have read it to the end (or you started at the end and don't have a clue what it's all about). But if you got this far, have studied the lessons diligently, and passed the test, you are probably feeling a "bit" like a stranger in your own land. That being the case, you might be a Carioca and not even know it. **Chocante!**

Anyway, I sincerely hope that reading this book has helped you get

over any rough times you might have had being a tourist in Rio. I never said it would be easy. Just remember: I would not trade this city for any place else in the world. It's my city and I love it.

So, if the thought of going back to wherever you came from isn't leaving you **numa boa, pô,** Rio could be your city, too. **Vamu nessa, mermão!** Call the folks, and put your house up for sale. And when you get back here, don't forget— **"Aparece em casa, viu?"**

I WANT YOU TO BE A CARIOCA

A B O U T   T H E   A U T H O R ⎯⎯⎯

Graphic designer, pianist, and mother of two
grown sons, Priscilla Goslin is a natural writer.
Born in a small mining town in the northern
woods of Minnesota, she found herself on
Ipanema beach for the first time at the ripe age
of six weeks. Having made Brazil her home
for more than thirty-four years, twenty-two
of which have been in Rio, Priscilla attributes
what she refers to as her cultural schizophre-
nia to the dichotomy created by her inherent
sense of order and her fascination for the
chaos only a passionate city such as Rio can
offer. As she says, "Being a tourist is a state
of mind, and I'll confess to often feeling like
a tourist in my own country. Now if I could
only figure out which country that is..."

When not catching waves off Barra beach or strumming his guitar, Carlos Carneiro can be found strapped into a cockpit in either Brazil, England, or the United States risking his neck as a race car driver. A bona fide Carioca—born and raised in Rio—his artistic talent was first recognized by his high school principal who, obviously not amused by Carlos' creativity, suspended him for drawing on the school's books, walls, and furniture. To this day Carlos still can't figure out how he got finagled into leaving his helmet on the shelf long enough to illustrate this book. But as he concedes, "I'd even draw pictures on Sugar Loaf Mountain if it would help finance the next racing season."